Emerson Andrews

Revival Songs

A New Collection of Hymns and Spiritual Songs for Closet and Family Worship,

Prayer, Conference, Revival and Protracted Meetings

Emerson Andrews

Revival Songs
A New Collection of Hymns and Spiritual Songs for Closet and Family Worship, Prayer, Conference, Revival and Protracted Meetings

ISBN/EAN: 9783337089610

Printed in Europe, USA, Canada, Australia, Japan

Cover: Foto ©Thomas Meinert / pixelio.de

More available books at **www.hansebooks.com**

REVIVAL SONGS:

A NEW COLLECTION OF

HYMNS AND SPIRITUAL SONGS

FOR

CLOSET AND FAMILY WORSHIP, PRAYER, CONFERENCE, REVIVAL AND PROTRACTED MEETINGS.

BY

REV. EMERSON ANDREWS, A. B., A. M.,
EVANGELIST.

"O, sing to the Lord a new song."
PSALMS xcvi. 1.

BOSTON:
PUBLISHED BY JAMES H. EARLE,
No. 96 WASHINGTON STREET.
1870.

PREFACE.

"WHAT! a new Hymn Book?" Yes, dear friend, just what you and every Christian need. For more than thirty years, while engaged almost constantly in revivals of religion, I have felt, like many others, the want of a *new* collection of Revival Hymns, comprising the best of the *Old* and the *New* songs; some in whole or in part, short and long, common and rare, original and select, in rich variety; adapted to add life, spirit, and power to closet and family devotions, and to promote the spirituality and efficiency of social, conference, prayer, and protracted meetings.

Here you have the long-desired compilation; much in a little; portable, choice, pure, *free*, instructive, devotional, spiritual. The "Old Hymns," so full of Bible truth, Christian experience, and sacred associations, are especially adapted to refresh, and vitalize, and sanctify God's people, and to direct and win sinners to Christ and heaven. So let it be. "Praise ye the Lord."

To glorify God and bless mankind, and be prepared to sing the New Song in heaven, is the object and prayer of your sincere friend,

EMERSON ANDREWS.

PHILADELPHIA, PA., July, 1870.

INDEX TO SUBJECTS.

1. AFFLICTIONS, 9, 27, 34, 137, 163, 212, 292, 298.
2. AWAKENING, 7, 14, 83, 171, 195, 214, 228.
3. BAPTISM, 13, 29, 71, 113, 140, 149, 205, 220, 274, 275.
4. COMFORTING, 10, 36, 56, 57, 74, 84, 134, 299.
5. CONVICTION, 18, 22, 88, 141, 231, 262, 295.
6. CONVERSION, 15, 25, 41, 44, 60, 95, 215, 224.
7. DOMESTIC, 26, 36, 61, 72, 78, 85, 175.
8. EXPERIENCE, 12, 28, 31, 35, 81, 90, 101, 112, 173.
9. FUNERALS, 21, 65, 91, 107, 157, 205, 223, 282.
10. GLORYING, 18, 63, 116, 139, 147, 194, 246, 298.
11. HEAVEN, 45, 106, 110, 138, 142, 236, 257, 297.
12. INVITING, 20, 38, 62, 93, 99, 103, 111, 207, 278.
13. JUDGMENT, 39, 47, 50, 75, 124, 271, 294.
14. LIBERTY, 126, 133, 146, 195, 198, 284, 290.
15. MISSIONS, 8, 140, 150, 210, 232, 289.
16. PRAYER, 3, 102, 144, 156, 166.
17. PARTING, 33, 37, 79, 118, 148, 273, 281.
18. REFORMS, 6, 165, 185, 192, 222, 287.
19. REVIVALS, 2, 7, 89, 96, 103, 115, 171, 174, 214.
20. SUPPER OF CHRIST, 12, 277, 278, 286, 292.
21. WORSHIP, 49, 68, 127, 151, 187, 239, 250, 252, 256, [338.

(5)

REVIVAL SONGS.

1. *Heavenly Love.* C. M.

1 COME, heavenly love, inspire my song
   With thine immortal flame,
And teach my heart, and teach my tongue,
   The Saviour's lovely name.

2 The Saviour! O, what endless charms
   Dwell in that blissful sound!
Its influence every fear disarms,
   And spreads delight around.

3 On thee alone my hope relies;
   Beneath thy cross I fall;
My Lord, my life, my sacrifice,
   My Saviour and my all!

2. *Voyage.* Stem the Storm. C. M.

1 O FOR a breeze of heavenly love,
   To waft my soul away
To the celestial world above,
   Where pleasures ne'er decay!

2 Eternal Spirit, deign to be
   My pilot here below,
To steer through life's tempestuous sea,
   Where winds do stormy blow.

3 From rocks of pride on either hand,
   From quicksands of despair,
O, guide me safe to Canaan's land,
   Through every latent snare.

4 Anchor me in that port above,
   On that celestial shore,
Where dashing billows never move,
   Where tempests never roar.

3.　　*Exhortation to Prayer.*　　**L. M.**

1 What various hinderances we meet
In coming to a mercy-seat!
Yet who, that knows the worth of prayer,
But wishes to be often there?

2 Prayer makes the darkened cloud withdraw;
Prayer climbs the ladder Jacob saw,
Gives exercise to faith and love,
Brings every blessing from above.

3 Restraining prayer, we cease to fight;
Prayer makes the Christian's armor bright;
And Satan trembles when he sees
The weakest saint upon his knees.

4 Have you no words? Ah, think again;
Words flow apace when you complain,
And fill your fellow-creature's ear
With the sad tale of all your care.

5 Were half the breath thus vainly spent
To Heaven in supplication sent,
Your cheerful songs would oftener be,
"Hear what the Lord has done for me!"

4.　　*Courage.*　　Valiant Soldier.　　**C. M.**

1 Ye valiant soldiers of the cross,
　Ye happy, praying band,
Though in this world you suffer loss,
　You'll reach fair Canaan's land.

Chorus. Let us never mind the scoffs nor the
　　　　frowns of the world,
　　For we all have the cross to bear;
　　It will only make the crown the
　　　　brighter to shine,
　　When we have the crown to wear.

2 All earthly pleasures we'll forsake
　When heaven appears in view,
In Jesus' strength we'll undertake
　To fight our passage through.

5. *Breathing after the Holy Spirit.* **C. M.**

1 Come, Holy Spirit, heavenly Dove,
  With all thy quickening powers,
Come, shed abroad a Saviour's love
  In these cold hearts of ours.

2 Look! how we grovel here below,
  Fond of these trifling toys!
Our souls can neither fly nor go,
  To reach eternal joys.

3 In vain we tune our formal songs;
  In vain we strive to rise;
Hosannas languish on our tongues,
  And our devotion dies.

4 Dear Lord, and shall we ever live
  At this poor dying rate, —
Our love so faint, so cold to thee,
  And thine to us so great?

5 Come, Holy Spirit, heavenly Dove,
  With all thy quickening powers,
Come, shed abroad a Saviour's love,
  And that shall kindle ours.

6. *Importance of Religion.* **C. M.**

1 Religion is the chief concern
  Of mortals here below;
May we its great importance learn,
  Its sovereign virtue know.

2 O, may our hearts, by grace renewed,
  Be our Redeemer's throne;
And be our stubborn wills subdued,
  His government to own.

3 Let deep repentance, faith, and love
  Be joined with godly fear,
And all our conversation prove
  Our hearts to be sincere.

4 Let lively hope our souls inspire;
  Let warm affections rise;
And may we wait with strong desire
  To mount above the skies.

7. *Sleepers.* Bower of Prayer. P. M.

1 Why sleep we, my brethren? come, let us arise;
O, why should we slumber in sight of the prize?
Salvation is nearer; our days are far spent;
O, let us be active; awake! and repent.

2 O, how can we slumber! the Master is come,
And calling on sinners to seek them a home;
The Spirit and Bride now in concert unite;
The weary they welcome, the careless invite.

3 O, how can we slumber! our foes are awake;
To ruin poor souls every effort they make;
To accomplish their object no means are untried;
The careless they comfort, the wakeful misguide.

4 O, how can we slumber, when so much was done
To purchase salvation by Jesus the Son!
Now mercy is proffered, and justice displayed;
Now God can be honored, and sinners be saved.

8. *Hinder me not.* Contrition. C. M.

1 In all my Lord's appointed ways
  My journey I'll pursue;
"Hinder me not," ye much-loved saints,
  For I must go with you.

2 Through floods and flames, if Jesus lead,
  I'll follow where he goes;
"Hinder me not," shall be my cry,
  Though earth and hell oppose.

3 Through duties, and through trials too,
  I'll go at his command;
"Hinder me not;" for I am bound
  To my Immanuel's land.

4 And, when my Saviour calls me home,
  Still this my cry shall be —
"Hinder me not;" come, welcome, death;
  I'll gladly go with thee.

9. *The Prodigal Son.*   Ortonville.   **C. M.**

1 Afflictions, though they seem severe,
  In mercy oft are sent;
They stopped the prodigal's career,
  And forced him to repent.

2 Although he no relenting felt
  Till he had spent his store,
His stubborn heart began to melt
  When famine pinched him sore.

3 "What have I gained by sin," he said,
  "But hunger, shame, and fear?
My father's house abounds with bread,
  While I am starving here.

4 "I'll go and tell him all I've done,
  And fall before his face;
Unworthy to be called his son,
  I'll seek a servant's place."

5 His father saw him coming back;
  He saw, and ran, and smiled,
And threw his arms around the neck
  Of his rebellious child.

6 "Father, I've sinned; but, O, forgive!"
  "Enough!" the father said;
"Rejoice, my house; my son's alive,
  For whom I mourned as dead.

7 "Now let the fatted calf be slain,
  And spread the news around;
My son was dead, but lives again,
  Was lost, but now is found."

8 'Tis thus the Lord his love reveals,
  To call poor sinners home;
More than a father's love he feels,
  And welcomes all that come.

10. *Precious Bible.* Greenville. 8s & 7s.

1 Precious Bible! what a treasure
    Does the word of God afford!
  All I want for life or pleasure,
    Food and medicine, shield and sword.
  Let the world account me poor;
  Having this, I need no more.

2 Food to which the world's a stranger
    Here my hungry soul enjoys;
  Of excess there is no danger;
    Though it fills, it never cloys.
  On a dying Christ I feed;
  He is meat and drink indeed.

3 When my faith is faint and sickly,
    Or when Satan wounds my mind,
  Cordials to revive me quickly,
    Healing medicines, here I find;
  To the promises I flee;
  Each affords a remedy.

11. *Pilgrims.* C. M.

1 Inquire, ye pilgrims, for the way
    That leads to Zion's hill,
  And thither set your steady face,
    With a determined will.

2 Invite the strangers all around
    Your pious march to join,
  And spread the sentiments you feel
    Of faith and love divine.

3 O, come, and to his temple haste,
    And seek his favor there;
  Before his footstool humbly bow,
    And pour your fervent prayer!

4 O, come, and join your souls to God
    In everlasting bands;
  Accept the blessings he bestows
    With thankful hearts and hands.

12.   *Repentance.   Loving Lamb.*   **C. M.**

1 Alas! and did my Saviour bleed?
    And did my Sovereign die?
  Would he devote that sacred head
    For such a wretch as I?

Chorus. O, the Lamb, the loving Lamb,
      The Lamb on Calvary;
    The Lamb that was slain,
    That liveth again,
      To intercede for me.

2 Was it for crimes that I have done
    He groaned upon the tree?
  Amazing pity! grace unknown!
    And love beyond degree!

3 Well might the sun in darkness hide,
    And shut his glories in,
  When God, the mighty Maker, died
    For man the creature's sin.

4 Thus might I hide my blushing face,
    While his dear cross appears,
  Dissolve my heart in thankfulness,
    And melt mine eyes to tears.

5 But drops of grief can ne'er repay
    The debt of love I owe;
  Here, Lord, I give myself away—
    'Tis all that I can do.

13.   *The Holy Spirit invoked.*   **L. M.**

1 Come, Holy Spirit, Dove divine,
  On these baptismal waters shine,
  And teach our hearts, in highest strain,
  To praise the Lamb for sinners slain.

2 We love thy name, we love thy laws,
  And joyfully embrace thy cause;
  We love thy cross, the shame, the pain,
  O Lamb of God, for sinners slain.

14. *The Awakened Sinner.* Ganges. 8s & 6s.

1 Awaked by Sinai's awful sound,
My soul in guilt and thrall I found,
 And knew not where to go.
O'erwhelmed in sin, with anguish slain,
"The sinner must be born again,
 Or sink in endless woe."

2 Amazed I stood, but could not tell
Which way to shun the gates of hell,
 For death and hell drew near;
I strove, indeed, but strove in vain;
"The sinner must be born again"
 Still sounded in my ear.

3 When to the law I trembling fled,
It poured its curses on my head;
 I no relief could find.
This fearful truth increased my pain;
"The sinner must be born again"
 O'erwhelmed my tortured mind.

4 Again did Sinai's thunder roll,
And guilt lay heavy on my soul,
 A vast, unwieldy load.
Alas! I read, and saw it plain,
"The sinner must be born again,
 Or drink the wrath of God."

5 The saints I heard with rapture tell
How Jesus conquered death and hell,
 And broke the fowler's snare;
Yet, when I found this truth remain,
"The sinner must be born again,"
 I sank in deep despair.

6 But while I thus in anguish lay,
Jesus of Nazareth passed that way,
 And felt his pity move.
The sinner, by his justice slain,
Now by his grace is born again,
 And sings redeeming love.

15. *Desiring Heaven.* **7s & 6s.**

1 O, when shall I see Jesus,
 And dwell with him above?
To drink the flowing fountains
 Of everlasting love?
When shall I be delivered
 From this vain world of sin,
And with my blessèd Jesus,
 Drink endless pleasures in?

2 Through grace I am determined
 To conquer, though I die;
And then away to Jesus
 On wings of love I'll fly.
Farewell to sin and sorrow;
 I bid you all adieu;
And you, my friends, prove faithful,
 And on your way pursue.

3 O, do not be discouraged,
 For Jesus is your friend,
And if you lack for knowledge,
 He'll not refuse to lend;
Neither will he upbraid you,
 Though ofttimes you request;
He'll give you grace to conquer,
 And take you home to rest.

16. *Christ knocking.* Hamburg. **L. M.**

1 Behold a stranger at the door!
He gently knocks — has knocked before;
Has waited long — is waiting still;
You treat no other friend so ill.

2 Admit him ere his anger burn;
His feet, departed, ne'er return;
Admit him, or the hour's at hand
You'll at his door rejected stand.

17. *Evangelist.*   I'm a Pilgrim.   **P. M.**

1 I'm a pilgrim, and I'm a stranger;
  I can tarry, I can tarry but a night;
  Do not detain me, for I am going
  To where the fountains are ever flowing.
  I'm a pilgrim, and I'm a stranger;
  I can tarry, I can tarry but a night.

2 There the glory is ever shining;
  I am longing, I am longing for the sight;
  Here in this country so dark and dreary
  I have been wandering forlorn and weary.
  I'm a pilgrim, and I'm a stranger;
  I can tarry, I can tarry but a night.

3 There's the city to which I journey;
  My Redeemer, my Redeemer is its light;
  There is no sorrow, nor any sighing,
  There is no sin there, nor any dying.
  I'm a pilgrim, and I'm a stranger;
  I can tarry, I can tarry but a night.

18.   *All due to God.*   **C. M.**

1 All that I *was*, my sin, my guilt,
   My death, was all my own;
  All that I *am* I owe to thee,
   My gracious God, alone.

2 The darkness of my former state,
   The bondage, all was mine;
  The light of life in which I walk,
   The liberty, is thine.

3 Thy grace first made me feel my sin,
   And taught me to believe;
  Then in believing, peace I found,
   And now I live, I live.

4 All that I am e'en here on earth,
   All that I hope to be
  When Jesus comes, and glory dawns,
   I owe it, Lord, to thee.

19. *The Cross.* **L. M.**

1 INSCRIBED upon the cross we see,
   In glowing letters, "God is love;"
 He bears our sins upon the tree;
   He brings us mercy from above.

2 The cross! it takes our guilt away;
   It holds the fainting spirit up;
 It cheers with hope the gloomy day,
   And sweetens every bitter cup;—

3 The balm of life, the cure of woe,
   The measure and the pledge of love,
 The sinner's refuge here below,
   The angel's theme in heaven above.

20. *Inviting.* EXPOSTULATION. **11s.**

1 O, TURN ye, O, turn ye, for why will you die,
 When God, in great mercy, is coming so nigh?
 Now Jesus invites you, the Spirit says, Come,
 And angels are waiting to welcome you home.

2 How vain the delusion, that while you delay,
 Your hearts may grow better by staying away!
 Come wretched, come starving, come just as you be,
 While streams of salvation are flowing so free.

3 And now Christ is ready your souls to receive,
 O, how can you question if you will believe?
 If sin is your burden, why will you not come?
 'Tis you he bids welcome; he bids you come home.

4 Come, give us your hand, and the Saviour your heart,
 And, trusting in heaven, we never shall part;
 O, how can we leave you? why will you not come?
 We'll journey together, and soon be at home.

21. *Pleading for Acceptance.* Surrender. **P. M.**

1 When thou, my righteous Judge, shalt come
To take thy ransomed people home,
  Shall I among them stand?
Shall such a worthless worm as I,
Who sometimes am afraid to die,
  Be found at thy right hand?

2 I love to meet thy people now,
Before thy feet with them to bow,
  Though vilest of them all;
But — can I bear the piercing thought? —
What if my name should be left out,
  When thou for them shalt call?

3 Prevent it, Lord, by thy rich grace;
Be thou my soul's sure hiding-place
  In this th' accepted day:
Thy pardoning voice, O, let me hear,
To still my unbelieving fear;
  Nor let me fall, I pray.

4 Let me among thy saints be found,
Whene'er th' archangel's trump shall sound,
  And see thy smiling face;
Then loudest of the crowd I'll sing,
While heaven's resounding mansions ring
  With shouts of sovereign grace.

22. *Free Grace.* **12s.**

1 The voice of free grace cries, Escape to the mountain;
For Adam's lost race Christ has opened a fountain;
For sins and uncleanness, for every transgression,
His blood flows most freely in streams of salvation.

Chorus.   Hallelujah to the Lamb! he hath purchased
      our pardon;
    We'll praise him again when we pass over
      Jordan.

2 Ye souls that are wounded, O, flee to the Saviour!
He calls you in mercy; 'tis infinite favor:
Your sins are increasing; escape to the mountain;
His blood can remove them, which flows from the fountain.

23. *Christian Heroism.* **10s & 11s.**

1 BEGONE, unbelief; my Saviour is near,
  And for my relief will surely appear;
  By prayer let me wrestle, and he will perform;
  With Christ in the vessel, I smile at the storm.

2 Though dark be my way, since he is my guide,
  'Tis mine to obey, and he will provide;
  Though cisterns be broken, and creatures all fail,
  The word he hath spoken will surely prevail.

3 His love in times past forbids me to think
  He'll leave me at last in sorrow to sink;
  Each sweet Ebenezer I have in review,
  Confirms his good pleasure to help me quite through.

4 Since all that I meet must work for my good,
  The bitter is sweet, the medicine's food:
  Though painful at present, 'twill cease before long,
  And then, O, how pleasant the conqueror's song.

24. *Christians.* Shall we meet. **8s & 7s.**

1 SHALL we meet beyond the river,
    Where the surges cease to roll,
  Where, in all the bright forever,
    Sorrow ne'er shall press the soul?

2 Shall we meet in that blest harbor,
    When our stormy voyage is o'er?
  Shall we meet and cast the anchor
    By the fair celestial shore?

3 Shall we meet with many a loved one,
    That was torn from our embrace?
  Shall we listen to their voices,
    And behold them face to face?

4 Shall we meet with Christ our Saviour,
    When he comes to claim his own?
  Shall we know his blessèd favor,
    And sit down upon his throne?

25. *Not ashamed of the Gospel.* **C. M.**

1 I'm not ashamed to own my Lord,
   Or to defend his cause,
 Maintain the honor of his word,
   The glory of his cross.

2 Jesus, my God, I know his name;
   His name is all my trust;
 Nor will he put my soul to shame,
   Nor let my hope be lost.

3 Firm as his throne his promise stands,
   And he can well secure
 What I've committed to his hands
   Till the decisive hour.

4 Then will he own my worthless name
   Before his Father's face,
 And in the New Jerusalem
   Appoint my soul a place.

26. *Witnesses.* I want to be an angel.

1 We all must speak for Jesus,
   Who hath redemption wrought,
 Who gave us peace and pardon,
   Which by his blood he bought.
 We all must speak for Jesus,
   To show how much we owe
 To Him who died to save us
   From death and endless woe.

2 We all must speak for Jesus,
   Where'er our lot may fall,
 To brothers, sisters, neighbors,
   In cottage and in hall.
 We all must speak for Jesus;
   The world in darkness lies;
 With him against the mighty
   Together we must rise.

27. *The Dying Christian.* All is well. **P. M.**

1 What's this that steals, that steals upon my frame?
 Is it death? Is it death?
That soon will quench, will quench this vital flame?
 Is it death? Is it death?
If this be death, I soon shall be
From every pain and sorrow free;
I shall the King of glory see.
 All is well, all is well.

2 Weep not, my friends, my friends, weep not for me;
 All is well, all is well.
My sins are pardoned, pardoned; I am free;
 All is well, all is well.
There's not a cloud that doth arise
To hide my Saviour from my eyes;
I soon shall mount the upper skies.
 All is well, all is well.

3 Hark, hark! my Lord and Master calls with grace;
 All is well, all is well.
I soon shall see, shall see his heavenly face;
 All is well, all is well.
Bright angels are from glory come;
They're round my bed, they're in my room,
They wait to waft my spirit home.
 All is well, all is well.

4 Hail, hail, all hail! all hail, ye blood washed throng,
 Saved by grace, saved by grace.
I've come to join, to join your rapturous song,
 Saved by grace, saved by grace.
All, all is peace and joy divine;
All heaven and glory now are mine;
O, hallelujah to the Lamb.
 All is well, all is well.

28. Good News. Will you go?

1 Whene'er we meet, you always say,
    What's the news? What's the news?
Pray, what's the order of the day?
    What's the news? What's the news?
O, I have got good news to tell!
My Saviour has done all things well,
And triumphed over death and hell,—
    That's the news! That's the news!

2 The Lamb was slain on Calvary,—
    That's the news! That's the news!
To set a world of sinners free,—
    That's the news! That's the news!
'Twas there his precious blood was shed,
But now he's risen from the dead,—
And all around his fame they spread, &c.

3 The Lord has pardoned all my sin,—
    That's the news! That's the news!
I feel the witness now within,—
    That's the news! That's the news!
And since he took my sins away,
And taught me how to watch and pray,
I'm happy now from day to day, &c.

4 And Christ the Lord can save you now,—
    That's the news! That's the news!
Your sinful hearts he can renew,—
    That's the news! That's the news!
This moment, if for sins you grieve,
This moment, if you do believe,
A full acquittal you'll receive, &c.

5 And then if any one should say,
    What's the news? What's the news?
O, tell them you've begun to pray,—
    That's the news! That's the news!
That you have joined the conquering band,
And now with joy, at God's command,
You're marching to the better land, &c.

29. *A great Question.* Wayfaring man. L. M.

1 Jesus, and shall it ever be —
A mortal man ashamed of thee!
Ashamed of thee, whom angels praise,
Whose glories shine through endless days?

2 Ashamed of Jesus! sooner far
Let evening blush to own a star;
He sheds the beams of light divine
O'er this benighted soul of mine.

3 Ashamed of Jesus! just as soon
Let midnight be ashamed of noon;
'Tis midnight with my soul till he,
Bright Morning Star, bids darkness flee.

4 Ashamed of Jesus, that dear friend
On whom my hopes of heaven depend!
No, when I blush, be this my shame,
That I no more revere his name.

5 Ashamed of Jesus! yes, I may,
When I've no guilt to wash away,
No tears to wipe, no good to crave,
No fears to quell, no soul to save.

6 Till then, — nor is my boasting vain, —
Till then I boast a Saviour slain;
And O, may this my glory be,
That Christ is not ashamed of me.

30. *Invitation.* Will you come. L. M.

1 Jesus, dear name, how sweet the sound,
Replete with balm for every wound!
His word declares his grace is free.
Come, needy sinner, come and see;
Come, guilty sinner, come and see, &c.

2 He left the shining courts on high,
Came to our world to bleed and die;
Jesus, the God, hung on the tree.
Come, helpless sinner, come and see;
Come, guilty sinner, come and see, &c.

1 I'm a pilgrim, and I'm a stranger;
 I can tarry, I can tarry but a night;
 Do not detain me, for I am going
 To where the fountains are ever flowing.

Chorus. I'm a pilgrim and I'm a stranger;
 I can tarry, I can tarry but a night.

2 There the glory is ever shining!
 O, my longing heart, my longing heart is there.
 Here in this country, so dark and dreary,
 I long have wandered forlorn and weary.

3 There's the city to which I journey;
 My Redeemer, my Redeemer is its light!
 There is no sorrow, nor any sighing,
 Nor any tears there, nor any dying!

4 Farewell, neighbors; with tears I've warned you;
 I must leave you, I must leave you and be gone!
 With this your portion, your hearts' desire,
 Why will you perish in raging fire?

32. *Praise to Jesus.* I do believe. C. M.

1 O for a thousand tongues to sing
  My dear Redeemer's praise!
 The glories of my God and King,
  The triumphs of his grace.

2 Jesus, the name that calms our fears,
  That bids our sorrows cease, —
 'Tis music in the sinner's ears;
  'Tis life, and health, and peace.

3 He breaks the power of reigning sin,
  He sets the prisoner free;
 His blood can make the foulest clean;
  His blood availed for me.

33. *Parting Song.* **P. M.**

1 FAREWELL, dear friends, I must be gone;
  I have no home or stay with you;
  I'll take my staff and travel on,
   Till I a better world do view.
Chorus. I'll march to Canaan's land,
   I'll land on Canaan's shore,
  Where pleasures never end,
   Where troubles come no more.
  Farewell, farewell, farewell,
  My loving friends, farewell.

2 Farewell, my friends, time rolls along,
   Nor waits for mortals' care or bliss;
  I leave you here, and travel on
   Till I arrive where Jesus is.

3 Farewell, my brethren in the Lord,
   To you I'm bound in cords of love;
  Yet we believe his gracious word,
   That soon we all shall meet above.

34. *Weeping Mary.* Martyn. **7s.**

1 MARY to the Saviour's tomb
   Hasted at the early dawn;
  Spice she brought, and rich perfume,
   But the Lord she loved had gone.
  For a while she lingering stood,
   Filled with sorrow and surprise,
  Trembling, while a crystal flood
   Issued from her weeping eyes.

2 But her sorrows quickly fled
   When she heard his welcome voice;
  Christ had risen from the dead;
   Now he bids her heart rejoice.
  What a change his word can make,
   Turning darkness into day!
  Ye who weep for Jesus' sake,
   He will wipe your tears away.

35. *Death welcome.* Frederick. **11s.**

1 I would not live alway: I ask not to stay
Where storm after storm rises dark o'er the way:
The few lurid mornings that dawn on us here
Are enough for life's woes, full enough for its cheer.

2 I would not live alway, thus fettered by sin,
Temptation without and corruption within:
E'en the rapture of pardon is mingled with fears,
And the cup of thanksgiving with penitent tears.

3 I would not live alway; no — welcome the tomb;
Since Jesus hath lain there, I dread not its gloom:
There sweet be my rest, till he bid me arise
To hail him in triumph descending the skies.

4 O, who would live alway, away from his God,
Away from yon heaven, that blissful abode,
Where the rivers of pleasure flow oe'r the bright plains,
And the noontide of glory eternally reigns?

5 There saints of all ages in harmony meet,
Their Saviour and brethren transported to greet,
While the anthems of rapture unceasingly roll,
And the smile of the Lord is the feast of the soul.

36. *God is Love.* Greenville. **8s & 7s.**

1 God is love; his mercy brightens
  All the path in which we rove;
 Bliss he wakes, and woe he lightens;
  God is wisdom, God is love.

2 Chance and change are busy ever;
  Man decays, and ages move;
 But his mercy waneth never;
  God is wisdom, God is love.

3 E'en the hour that darkest seemeth
  Will his changeless goodness prove;
 From the gloom his brightness streameth;
  God is wisdom, God is love.

37. *The Bower of Prayer.* **11s.**

1 To leave my dear friends, and with neighbors to part,
And go from my home, it afflicts not my heart,
Like the thought of absenting myself for a day,
From that blessèd retreat where I've chosen to pray.

2 Sweet bower, where the pine and the poplar have spread,
And woven their branches, a roof o'er my head,
How oft have I knelt on the evergreen there,
And poured out my soul to my Saviour in prayer!

3 How sweet were the zephyrs perfumed by the pine,
The ivy, the balsam, and wild eglantine!
But sweeter, O sweeter, superlative were
The joys that I tasted in answer to prayer!

4 For Jesus, my Saviour, oft deignèd to meet,
And bless with his presence my humble retreat,
Oft filled me with raptures and blessedness there,
Inditing, in heaven's own language, my prayer.

5 Dear bower, I must leave you, and bid you adieu,
And pay my devotions in parts that are new,
Well knowing my Saviour resides everywhere,
And can in all places give answer to prayer.

6 Although I shall never revisit the shade,
Yet oft shall I think of the vows I have made;
And while at a distance, my mind will repair
To the place where my Saviour first answered my prayer.

38. *Expostulation.* 8s & 7s.

1 Now the Saviour standeth pleading,
 At the sinner's bolted heart;
Now in heaven he's interceding,
 Undertaking sinners' part.

Chorus. Sinners, can you hate this Saviour?
 Will you thrust him from your arms?
Once he died for your behavior;
 Now he call you to his arms.

2 Now he pleads his sweat and blood-shed,
 Shows his wounded hands and feet;
Father, save them, though they're blood red,
 Raise them to a heavenly seat.

3 Sinners, hear your God and Saviour,
 Hear his gracious voice to-day;
Turn from all your vain behavior;
 O; repent, return, and pray.

4 O, be wise before you languish
 On the bed of dying strife;
Endless joy, or dreadful anguish,
 Turn upon the events of life.

5 Now he's waiting to be gracious,
 Now he stands and looks on thee;
See what kindness, love, and pity
 Shine around on you and me.

6 Open now your hearts before him,
 Bid the Saviour welcome in;
Now receive, and O, adore him,
 Take a full discharge from sin.

7 Come, for all things now are ready;
 Yet there's room for many more;
O, ye blind, ye lame, and needy,
 Come to wisdom's boundless store.

39. *The Final Day.* **C. M.**

1 That awful day will surely come, —
    Th' appointed hour makes haste, —
When I must stand before my Judge,
    And pass the solemn test.

Chorus. The judgment day is rolling on,
    The judgment day is rolling on
    The judgment day is rolling on.
        Prepare to meet thy God.

2 Thou lovely Chief of all my joys,
    Thou Sovereign of my heart,
How could I bear to hear thy voice
    Pronounce the sound, "Depart!"

3 O, tell me that my worthless name
    Is graven on thy hands;
Show me some promise in thy book,
    Where my salvation stands.

40. *Confiding.* Hamburg. **L. M.**

1 Just as I am, without one plea
But that thy blood was shed for me,
And that thou bid'st me come to thee,
    O Lamb of God, I come, I come.

2 Just as I am, and waiting not
To rid my soul of one dark blot,
To thee whose blood can cleanse each spot,
    O Lamb of God, I come, I come.

3 Just as I am, thou wilt receive,
Wilt welcome, pardon, cleanse, relieve,
Because thy promise I believe:
    O Lamb of God, I come, I come.

4 Just as I am, thy love unknown
Has broken every barrier down;
Now to be thine, yea, thine alone,
    O Lamb of God, I come, I come.

41.   *Sweet Home.*   11s.

1 An alien from God, and a stranger to grace,
I wandered through earth, its gay pleasures to trace;
In the pathway of sin I continued to roam,
Unmindful, alas! that it led me from home.
    Home, home, sweet, sweet home!
    O Saviour, direct me to heaven, my home.

2 The pleasures of earth I have seen fade away;
They bloom for a season, but soon they decay;
But pleasures more lasting in Jesus are given —
Salvation on earth and a mansion in heaven.
    Home, home, sweet, sweet home!
    The saints in those mansions are ever at home.

3 Farewell, vain amusements! my follies, adieu!
While Jesus, and heaven, and glory I view,
I feast on the pleasures that flow from his throne,
The foretaste of heaven, sweet heaven, my home.
    Home, home, sweet, sweet home!
    O, when shall I share the fruition of home!

4 The days of my exile are passing away;
The time is approaching when Jesus will say,
"Well done, faithful servant; sit down on my throne,
And dwell in my presence forever at home."
    Home, home, sweet, sweet home!
    O, there I shall rest with the Saviour at home.

5 Affliction, and sorrow, and death shall be o'er;
The saints shall unite to be parted no more;
There loud hallelujahs fill heaven's high dome;
They dwell with the Saviour forever at home.
    Home, home, sweet, sweet home!
    They dwell with the Saviour forever at home.

42. *The Soldier's Song.* Bower. 11s.

1 I HAVE fought the good fight, I have finished
my race,
And thee, O my Saviour, I soon shall embrace;
They may torture this body — my spirit is free,
And the billows of death shall but waft it to thee.

2 Let thy strength, Lord, but gird me, thy smile
be but mine,
And my soul on thy faithfulness firmly recline,
The dungeon, the sword, or the stake, I can dare,
And in transports expire, if my Jesus be there.

3 United in sufferings, — the promise is clear, —
I shall with my Jesus in glory appear;
Out of great tribulation in triumph I go,
With my robe washed in blood, and made whiter
than snow.

43. *Precious Promises.* Bower. 11s.

1 How firm a foundation, ye saints of the Lord,
Is laid for your faith in his excellent word!
What more can he say than to you he hath
said —
You, who unto Jesus for refuge have fled?

2 In every condition, — in sickness, in health,
In poverty's vale, or abounding in wealth,
At home and abroad, on the land, on the sea, —
As thy days may demand shall thy strength
ever be.

3 Fear not; I am with thee; O, be not dis-
mayed;
I, I am thy God, and will still give thee aid;
I'll strengthen thee, help thee, and cause thee to
stand,
Upheld by my righteous, omnipotent hand.

4 Even down to old age, all my people shall prove
My sovereign, eternal, unchangeable love;
And when hoary hairs shall their temples adorn,
Like lambs they shall still in my bosom be borne.

44. *The Female Pilgrim.* P. M.

1 Whither goest thou, pilgrim stranger,
  Wandering through this gloomy vale?
 Know'st thou not 'tis full of danger,
  And will not thy courage fail?

Chorus. O, I'm bound for the kingdom;
  Will you go to glory with me?
  Hallelujah! Praise ye the Lord.

2 Pilgrim thou dost justly call me,
  Travelling through this lonely void;
 But no ill shall e'er befall me,
  While I'm blessed with such a guide.

3 Such a guide! No guide attends thee;
  Hence for thee my fears arise;
 If some guardian power defend thee,
  'Tis unseen by mortal eyes.

4 Yes, unseen; but still, believe me,
  Such a guide my steps attend;
 He'll in every strait relieve me,
  He will guide me to the end.

5 Pilgrim, see that stream before thee,
  Darkly rolling through the vale;
 Should its boisterous waves roll o'er thee,
  Would not then thy courage fail?

6 No; that stream has nothing frightful;
  To its brink my steps I'll bend;
 Thence to plunge 'twill be delightful;
  There my pilgrimage will end.

7 While I gazed, with speed surprising,
  Down the vale she plunged from sight;
 Gazing still, I saw her rising,
  Like an angel clothed in light!

Chorus. O, she's gone to the kingdom;
  Will you follow her to glory?
  Hallelujah! Praise ye the Lord.

45.   *The Heavenly Canaan.*   Auld Lang Syne.   C. M.

1 There is a land of pure delight,
    Where saints immortal reign;
 Eternal day excludes the night,
    And pleasures banish pain.

2 There everlasting spring abides,
    And never-fading flowers:
 Death, like a narrow sea, divides
    That heavenly land from ours.

3 O, could we make our doubts remove, —
    Those gloomy doubts that rise, —
 And see the Canaan that we love
    With unbeclouded eyes, —

4 Could we but climb where Moses stood,
    And view the landscape o'er, —
 Not Jordan's stream nor death's cold flood
    Should fright us from the shore.

46.   *The Hope of Heaven.*   Pisgah.   C. M.

1 When I can read my title clear
    To mansions in the skies,
 I'll bid farewell to every fear,
    And wipe my weeping eyes.

2 Should earth against my soul engage,
    And fiery darts be hurled,
 Then I can smile at Satan's rage,
    And face a frowning world.

3 Let cares, like a wild deluge, come,
    And storms of sorrow fall,
 May I but safely reach my home,
    My God, my heaven, my all,

4 There shall I bathe my weary soul
    In seas of heavenly rest,
 And not a wave of trouble roll
    Across my peaceful breast.

47. *The Warning Voice.* Bunker Hill. **C. M.**

1 Ah, guilty sinner, ruined by transgression,
  What shall thy doom be, when array'd in terror,
  God shall command thee, covered with pollution,
    Up to the judgment?

2 Wilt thou escape from his omniscient notice,
  Fly to the caverns, court annihilation?
  Vain thy presumption, justice still shall triumph
    In thy destruction.

3 Stop, thoughtless sinner, stop a while and ponder
  Ere death arrest thee, and the Judge, in vengeance,
  Hurl from his presence thine affrighted spirit
    Swift to perdition.   [him;

4 Oft has he called thee, but thou wouldst not hear
  Mercies and judgments have alike been slighted,
  Yet he is gracious, and with arms unfolded
    Waits to embrace thee.

5 Come, then, poor sinner, come away this mo-
  Just as you are, come, filthy and polluted, [ment
  Come to the fountain open for uncleanness;
    Jesus invites you.

6 But, if you trifle with his gracious message,
  Cleave to the world, and love its guilty pleasures,
  Mercy, grown weary, shall in righteous judgment
    Quit you forever.

7 Then you shall call, but he will not regard you,
  Seek for his favor, yet shall never find it,
  Cry to the rocks to hide you from his presence,
    Deep in their caverns.

8 Where the worm dies not, and the fire eternal
  Fills the lost soul with anguish and with terror,
  There shall the sinner spend a long forever,
    Dying unpardoned.

9 O, guilty sinner, hear the voice of warning;
  Fly to the Saviour, and embrace his pardon;
  So shall your spirit meet, with joy triumphant,
    Death and the judgment.

48. *The Hiding-Place.* Bonnie Doon. L. M.

1 Hail, sovereign love, that first began
The scheme to rescue fallen man!
Hail, matchless, free, eternal grace,
That gave my soul a hiding-place!

2 Against the God, that built the sky,
I fought with hands uplifted high,
Despised the mansions of his grace,
Too proud to seek a hiding-place.

3 Enwrapt in dark, Egyptian night,
And fond of darkness more than light,
Madly I ran the sinful race,
Secure without a hiding-place.

4 But lo! the eternal counsel ran,
" Almighty Love, arrest the man ;"
I felt the arrows of distress,
And found I had no hiding-place.

5 Vindictive Justice stood in view;
To Sinai's fiery mount I flew;
But Justice cried, with frowning face,
This mountain is no hiding-place.

6 But lo! a heavenly voice I heard,
And Mercy's angel soon appeared,
Who led me, on a pleasing pace,
To Jesus Christ, my hiding-place.

7 On him Almighty vengeance fell,
Which must have sunk a world to hell;
He bore it for his chosen race,
And thus became their hiding-place.

49. *Spiritual Improvement.* I love Jesus. 8s & 7s.

1 In thy name, O Lord, assembling,
  We, thy people, now draw near;
Teach us to rejoice with trembling;
  Speak, and let thy servants hear,—
    Hear with meekness,—
  Hear thy word with godly fear.

50. *Christ's Coming.* Nettleton. 8s & 7s.

1 Don't you see my Jesus coming?
  Don't you see him in yon cloud,
With ten thousand angels round him?
  How they do my Jesus crowd!

2 Don't you see his arms extended?
  Don't you hear his charming voice?
Loving hearts beat high for glory,
  O, my Jesus is my choice.

3 Don't you see the saints ascending?
  Hear them shouting through the air?
Jesus smiling, trumpets sounding,
  Now his glory they shall share.

4 Don't you see the heavens open,
  And the saints in glory there?
Shouts of triumph bursting round you?
  Glory, glory, glory here!

5 Come, backsliders, tho' you've pierced him,
  And have caused his church to mourn,
Yet you may regain free pardon,
  If you will to him return.

6 There we'll range the fields of pleasure
  By our dear Redeemer's side,
Shouting, Glory, glory, glory,
  While eternal ages glide.

51. *Consolation.* Cross and Crown. C. M.

1 My pilgrimage will shortly end
  Here in this world of sin:
To me thy hand will you now lend,
  And always be my friend.
Be with me when I come to die,
  O, that's the joy for me;
And fill me with that joy on high,
  O, that's the joy for me.

52. *Holy Voyage.* Homeward Bound. **P. M.**

1 Out on an ocean all boundless we ride —
  We're homeward bound;
 Tossed on the waves of a rough, restless tide —
  We're homeward bound;
 Far from the safe, quiet harbor we've rode,
 Seeking our Father's celestial abode,
 Promise of which on us each he bestowed —
  We're homeward bound.

2 We'll tell the world, as we journey along,
  We're homeward bound;
 Try to persuade them to enter our throng —
  We're homeward bound;
 Come, trembling sinner, forlorn and oppressed,
 Join in our number; O come and be blest;
 Journey with us to the mansions of rest —
  We're homeward bound.

3 Into the harbor of heaven now we glide —
  We're home at last;
 Softly we drift on its bright silver tide —
  We're home at last;
 Glory to God, all our dangers are o'er;
 We stand secure on the glorified shore;
 Glory to God, we will shout evermore;
  We're home at last.

53. *The Church victorious.* **11s. P. M.**

1 Daughter of Zion, awake from thy sadness;
  Awake, for thy foes shall oppress thee no more:
 Bright o'er thy hills dawns the daystar of gladness;
  Arise, for the night of thy sorrow is o'er.

2 Daughter of Zion, the power that hath saved thee
  Extolled with the harp and the timbrel should be;
 Shout, for the foe is destroyed that enslaved thee,
  Th' oppressor is vanquished, and Zion is free.

54. *Blood of Jesus.* I do believe. **C. M.**

1 There is a fountain filled with blood,
  Drawn from Immanuel's veins,
 And sinners, plunged beneath that flood,
  Lose all their guilty stains.

2 The dying thief rejoiced to see
  That fountain, in his day;
 O, may I there, though vile as he,
  Wash all my sins away.

3 Thou dying Lamb, thy precious blood
  Shall never lose its power,
 Till all the ransomed church of God
  Are saved, to sin no more.

4 E'er since, by faith, I saw the stream
  Thy flowing wounds supply,
 Redeeming love has been my theme,
  And shall be, till I die.

5 And when this feeble, faltering tongue
  Lies silent in the grave,
 Then, in a nobler, sweeter song,
  I'll sing thy power to save.

55. *All of Grace.* Jesus paid it all. **7s & 6s.**

1 Nothing, either great or small,
  Remains for me to do;
 Jesus died, and paid it all,—
  Yes, all the debt I owe.
   Jesus paid it all, &c.

2 Till to Jesus' work you cling
  Alone by simple faith,
 "Doing" is a deadly thing;
  All "doing" ends in death.

3 Cast your deadly "doing" down,
  Down, all at Jesus' feet;
 Stand in him, in him alone,
  All glorious and complete.

56. *The Holy Feast.* Praise God. 7s.

1 Come and taste, along with me,
Consolation running free
From my Father's wealthy throne,
Sweeter than the honey-comb.

Chorus. I'll praise God, and you'll praise God,
And we'll all praise God together;
I'll praise the Lord for the work that
he has done,
And we'll bless his name forever.

2 Why should Christians feast alone?
Two are better far than one;
The more that come with free good will
Makes the banquet sweeter still.

3 Now I go to heaven's door,
Asking for a little more;
Jesus gives a double share,
Calling me his chosen heir.

4 Goodness running like a stream
Through the New Jerusalem,
By its constant breaking forth
Sweetens earth and heaven both.

5 Saints in glory sing aloud
To behold an heir of God
Coming in at heaven's door,
Making up the number more.

6 Heaven here and heaven there;
Comforts flowing everywhere;
This I boldly can attest,
That my soul has got a taste.

7 Now I go rejoicing home
From the banquet of perfume,
Gleaning manna on the road,
Dropping from the mount of God.

57. *The Eden of Love.* 12s & 11s.

1 How sweet to reflect on those joys that await me
   In yon blissful region, the haven of rest,
Where glorified spirits with welcome shall greet me
   And lead me to mansions prepared for the blest!
Encircled in light, and with glory enshrouded,
My happiness perfect, my mind's sky unclouded,
I'll bathe in the ocean of pleasure unbounded,
   And range with delight through the Eden of love.

2 While angelic legions, with harps tuned celestial,
   Harmoniously join in the concert of praise,
The saints, as they flock from the regions terrestrial,
   In loud hallelujahs their voices will raise;
Then songs to the Lamb shall reëcho through heaven;
My soul will respond, "To Immanuel be given
All glory, all honor, all might, and dominion,
   Who brought us through grace to the Eden of love."

58. *Sorrows of Christ.* St. Denis. 11s.

1 Thou sweet gliding Kedron, by thy silver streams,
Our Saviour at midnight, when moonlight's pale beams
Shone bright on the waters, would frequently stray,
And lose, in thy murmurs, the toils of the day.

2 O garden of Olivet, thou dear honored spot,
The fame of thy wonders shall ne'er be forgot,
The theme most transporting to seraphs above —
The triumph of sorrow, the triumph of love!

3 Come, saints, and adore him; come, bow at his feet;
O, give him the glory, the praise that is meet;
Let joyful hosannas unceasing arise,
And join the full chorus that gladdens the skies.

59. *The converted Thief.* I do believe. **C. M.**

1 As on the cross the Saviour hung,
    And wept, and bled, and died,
He poured salvation on a wretch
    That languished at his side.

2 His crimes, with inward grief and shame,
    The penitent confessed,
Then turned his dying eyes to Christ,
    And thus his prayer addressed:—

3 "Jesus, thou Son and Heir of heaven!
    Thou spotless Lamb of God!
I see thee bathed in sweat and tears,
    And weltering in thy blood.

4 "Yet quickly, from these scenes of woe,
    In triumph thou shalt rise,
Burst through the gloomy shades of death,
    And shine above the skies.

5 "Amid the glories of that world,
    Dear Saviour, think on me,
And in the victories of thy death
    Let me a sharer be."

60. *Unspeakable Love.* Bower. **11s.**

1 I LOVE thee, I love thee, I love thee, my Lord;
I love thee, my Saviour, I love thee, my God;
I love thee, I love thee, and that thou dost know;
But how much I love thee I never can show.

2 I'm happy, I'm happy, O wondrous account!
My joys are immortal; I stand on the mount!
I gaze on my treasure, and long to be there
With Jesus and angels, my kindred so dear.

3 O Jesus, my Saviour, with thee I am blest!
My life and salvation, my joy and my rest!
Thy name be my theme, and thy love be my song;
Thy grace shall inspire both my heart and my tongue.

61. *Star in the East.* 11s & 10s. P.M.

1 Hail the blest morn! see the great Mediator
  Down from the regions of glory descend!
 Shepherds, go worship the Babe in the manger:
  Lo! for his guard, the bright angels attend.

Chorus. Brightest and best of the sons of the morning,
  Dawn on our darkness, and lend us thine aid;
 Star in the east, the horizon adorning,
  Guide where our infant Redeemer is laid.

2 Cold on his cradle the dew drops are shining;
  Low lies his head with the beasts of the stall;
 Angels adore him, in slumbers reclining,
  Wise men and shepherds before him do fall.

3 Say, shall we yield him, in costly devotion,
  Odors of Edon and offerings divine,
 Gems from the mountains, and pearls from the ocean,
  Myrrh from the forest, and gold from the mine?

4 Vainly we offer each ample oblation,
  Vainly with gold would his favor secure;
 Richer by far is the heart's adoration;
  Dearer to God are the prayers of the poor.

62. *Invitation to the Mercy-Seat.* 11s. & 10s.

1 Come, ye disconsolate, where'er ye languish;
  Come to the mercy-seat, fervently kneel;
 Here bring your wounded hearts, here tell your anguish;
  Earth has no sorrow that heaven cannot heal.

2 Joy of the desolate, light of the straying,
  Hope of the penitent, fadeless and pure,
 Here speaks the Comforter, tenderly saying,
  Earth has no sorrow that heaven cannot cure.

3 Here see the bread of life; see waters flowing
  Forth from the throne of God, pure from above;
 Come to the feast of love, come, ever knowing
  Earth has no sorrow but heaven can remove.

63. *The Spiritual Coronation.* Coronation. C. M.

1 ALL hail the power of Jesus' name!
  Let angels prostrate fall;
Bring forth the royal diadem,
  And crown him Lord of all.

2 Ye chosen seed of Israel's race,—
  A remnant weak and small,—
Hail him who saves you by his grace,
  And crown him Lord of all.

3 Ye Gentile sinners, ne'er forget
  The wormwood and the gall;
Go, spread your trophies at his feet,
  And crown him Lord of all.

4 Let every kindred, every tribe,
  On this terrestrial ball,
To him all majesty ascribe,
  And crown him Lord of all.

5 O that, with yonder sacred throng,
  We at his feet may fall!
We'll join the everlasting song,
  And crown him Lord of all.

64. *Our Shepherd.* Bower. 11s.

1 THE Lord is our shepherd, our guardian and guide;
Whatever we want he will kindly provide;
To the sheep of his pasture his mercies abound;
His care and protection his flock will surround.

2 The Lord is our shepherd; what, then, shall we fear?
What danger can frighten us while he is near?
Not when the time calls us to walk through the vale
Of the shadow of death, shall our hearts ever fail.

3 The Lord is become our salvation and song;
His blessings have followed us all our life long;
His name will we praise while we have any breath;
Be cheerful in life, and be happy in death.

65. *Eternity.*   Ice and Snow. **7s.**

1 O, ye young, ye gay and proud,
You must die and wear the shroud;
Time will rid you of your bloom,
Death will drag you to the tomb;
Then you'll cry and want to be
    Happy in eternity.

2 Say? will you go to heaven or hell?
One you must, and there to dwell;
Christ will come, and quickly too;
I must see him, so must you;
Then you'll cry and want to be
    Happy in eternity.

3 The white throne will soon appear;
All the world must then draw near;
Sinners must be driven down;
Saints will wear a starry crown;
Then you'll cry and want to be
    Happy in eternity.

4 O, ye mourning, sinking souls,
See beyond the torrent rolls;
Now believe with all your might;
Christ will make your garments white;
Then you'll ever with him be
    Happy in eternity.

66.   *Worship.*   Rolland. **L. M.**

1 Jesus, where'er thy people meet,
There they behold thy mercy-seat;
Where'er they seek thee, thou art found,
And every place is hallowed ground.

2 Here may we prove the power of prayer
To strengthen faith and sweeten care,
To teach our faint desires to rise,
And bring all heaven before our eyes.

67. *To-day.* Will you go? **L. M.**

1 To-day, if you will hear his voice,
　　　Will you go? Will you go?
　Now is the time to make your choice;
　　　Will you go? Will you go?
　Say, will you be forever blest,
　And with the glorious Jesus rest?
　And with the glorious Jesus rest?
　　　Will you go? Will you go?

2 Will you be saved from guilt and pain?
　Will you with Christ forever reign?
　Say, will you to Mount Zion go?
　Say, will you have this Christ, or no?

3 Come, blooming youth, for ruin bound,
　Obey the gospel's joyful sound;
　Come, go with us, and you shall prove
　The joys of Christ's redeeming love.

4 Behold, he's waiting at your door!
　Make now your choice; O, halt no more;
　Say, sinner, say, what will you do?
　Say, will you have this Christ, or no?

5 Your sports, and all your glittering toys,
　Compared to our celestial joys,
　Like momentary dreams appear;
　Come, go with us — your souls are dear.

6 Why rush in carnal pleasures on?
　Why madly plunge in sorrow down?
　Say, without Christ what can you do?
　Say, will you have this Christ, or no?

7 O, must we bid you all farewell,
　We bound to heaven, and you to hell?
　Still God may hear us while we pray,
　And change you ere that burning day.

8 Once more we ask you in his name;
　We know his love remains the same:
　Say, will you to Mount Zion go?
　Say, will you have this Christ, or no?

68. *Sweet Hour of Prayer.* **D. L. M.**

1 Sweet hour of prayer! sweet hour of prayer!
  That calls me from a world of care,
  And bids me at my Father's throne
  Make all my wants and wishes known!
  In seasons of distress and grief
  My soul has often found relief,
  And oft escaped the tempter's snare,
  By thy return, sweet hour of prayer.

2 Sweet hour of prayer! sweet hour of prayer!
  Thy wings shall my petition bear
  To Him whose truth and faithfulness
  Engage the waiting soul to bless;
  And since he bids me seek his face,
  Believe his word, and trust his grace,
  I'll cast on him my every care,
  And wait for thee, sweet hour of prayer.

3 Sweet hour of prayer! sweet hour of prayer!
  May I thy consolation share;
  Till from Mount Pisgah's lofty height
  I view my home, and take my flight:
  This robe of flesh I'll drop, and rise
  To seize the everlasting prize,
  And shout, while passing through the air,
  Farewell, farewell, sweet hour of prayer!

69. *The Care of the Good Shepherd.* **11s.**

1 The Lord is my Shepherd; no want shall I know;
  I feed in green pastures, safe folded to rest;
  He leadeth my soul where the still waters flow,
  Restores me when wandering, redeems when oppressed.

2 Thro' the valley and shadow of death though I stray,
  Since thou art my Guardian, no evil I fear;
  Thy rod shall defend me, thy staff be my stay;
  No harm can befall with my Comforter near.

70.   *The Atonement.*   P. M.

1 Saw ye my Saviour — saw ye my Saviour, —
Saw ye my Saviour and God?
O, he died on Calvary,
To atone for you and me,
And to purchase our pardon with blood.

2 He was extended — he was extended,
Painfully nailed to the cross;
Here he bowed his head and died;
Thus my Lord was crucified,
To atone for a world that was lost.

3 Jesus hung bleeding — Jesus hung bleeding,
Three dreadful hours in pain;
And the solid rocks were rent,
Through creation's vast extent,
When the Jews crucified the God-man.

4 Darkness prevailed — darkness prevailed —
Darkness prevailed o'er the land;
And the sun refused to shine,
When his majesty divine
Was derided, insulted, and slain.

5 When it was finished — when it was finished,
And the atonement was made,
He was taken by the great,
And embalmed with spices sweet,
And was in a new sepulchre laid.

6 Hail, mighty Saviour — hail, mighty Saviour,
Prince, and the author of peace;
O, he burst the bars of death,
And, triumphant, from the earth
He ascended to mansions of bliss.

7 There interceding — there interceding,
Pleading that sinners may live,
Crying, "Father, I have died,
O, behold my hands and side;
O, forgive them, I pray thee, forgive."

8 "I will forgive them — I will forgive them
When they repent and believe;
Let them now return to thee,
And be reconciled to me,
And salvation they all shall receive.'

71. *Christ's Baptism.* Bonnie Doon. **P. M.**

1 In Jordan's tide the Baptist stands,
  Immersing the repenting Jews:
The Son of God the rite demands:
  Nor dares the holy man refuse
To plunge his Lord beneath the wave,
The emblem of his future grave.

2 Admire, ye heavens! the Saviour lies
  In deeps, concealed from human view:
Ye saints, behold him sink and rise;
  A fit example this for you.
The sacred records, while you read,
Call you to imitate the deed.

3 Thus the eternal Father spoke,
  Who shakes creation with a nod;
Through parting skies the accents broke,
  And bade us hear the Son of God;
O, hear the joyful word to-day!
Hear, all ye nations, and obey!

72. *Responsibility.* Kentucky. **S. M.**

1 A charge to keep I have,
  A God to glorify,
A never-dying soul to save,
  And fit it for the sky.

2 To serve the present age,
  My calling to fulfil,
O, may it all my powers engage,
  To do my Master's will.

3 Arm me with jealous care,
  As in thy sight to live;
And O, thy servant, Lord, prepare,
  A strict account to give!

4 Help me to watch and pray
  And on thyself rely,
Assured, if I my trust betray,
  I shall forever die.

73. *The Joy of Assurance.* 6s & 9s. P. M.

1 O, HOW happy are they
 Who the Saviour obey,
And whose treasures are laid up above!
 Tongue cannot express
 The sweet comfort and peace
Of a soul in its earliest love.

2 That sweet comfort was mine,
 When the favor divine
I first found in the blood of the Lamb;
 When my heart first believed,
 O, what joy I received!
What a heaven in Jesus's name!

3 'Twas a heaven below
 The Redeemer to know;
And the angels could do nothing more
 Than to fall at his feet,
 And the story repeat,
And the Lover of sinners adore.

4 Jesus, all the day long,
 Was my joy and my song;
O, that all his salvation might see!
 He hath loved me, I cried,
 He hath suffered and died
To redeem such a rebel as me.

74. *Rejoicing.* Triumph. 10s.

1 JOYFULLY, joyfully onward I move,
Bound for the land of bright spirits above;
Angelic choristers sing as I come,
"Joyfully, joyfully haste to thy home."
Soon, with my pilgrimage ended below,
Home to that land of delight will I go;
Pilgrim and stranger no more shall I roam,
Joyfully, joyfully resting at home.

75. *Judgment Hymn.* 11s & 8s.

1 O, THERE will be mourning, mourning, mourning, mourning,
O, there will be mourning, at the judgment-seat of Christ.
    Parents and children there will part,
    Parents and children there will part,
    Parents and children there will part,
    Will part to meet no more.

2 O, there will be mourning, &c.
    Wives and husbands there will part, &c.

3 O, there will be mourning, &c.
    Brothers and sisters there will part, &c.

4 O, there will be mourning, &c.
    Friends and neighbors there will part, &c.

5 O, there will be mourning, &c.
    Pastors and people there will part, &c.

6 O, there will be mourning, &c.
    Devils and sinners there will meet, &c.
    Will meet to part no more.

7. O, there will be shouting, &c.
    Saints and angels there will meet, &c.
    Will meet to part no more.

76. *Jesus precious.* 11s.

1 O JESUS, my Saviour, to thee I submit,
With love and thanksgiving fall down at thy feet,
In sacrifice offer my soul, flesh, and blood;
Thou art my Redeemer, my Lord, and my God.

2 All human expressions are empty and vain;
They cannot give voice to this heavenly flame;
I'm sure, if the tongue of an angel were mine,
I could not this mystery completely define.

3 I'm happy, my Saviour, and that past account;
My joys are immortal; I stand on the mount;
I gaze on my treasure, and long to be there,
With Jesus, and angels, and kindred so dear.

77. *Christ in the Garden.* Bower. **11s.**

1 While nature was sinking in stillness to rest,
  The last beams of daylight shone dim in the west;
 O'er fields by the moonlight, to lonely retreat,
 In deep meditation, I wandered to weep.

2 While passing a garden, as I paused to hear
  A voice, faint and faltering, from one that was there,
 The voice of the mourner affected my heart,
 While pleading in anguish the poor sinner's part.

3 In offering to Heaven his pitying prayer,
 He spake of the torments the sinner must bear;
 His life as a ransom he offered to give,
 That sinners redeemed in glory might live.

4 I listened a moment, and then turned to see
  What man of compassion this stranger could be;
 When, lo! I discovered, knelt on the cold green,
 The loveliest being that ever was seen.

78. *The Earnest of Heaven.* Ortonville. **C. M.**

1 Why should the children of a King
  Go mourning all their days?
 Great Comforter, descend, and bring
  Some tokens of thy grace.

2 Dost thou not dwell in all thy saints,
  And seal them heirs of heaven?
 When wilt thou banish my complaints,
  And show my sins forgiven?

3 Thou art the earnest of his love,
  The pledge of joys to come;
 And thy soft wings, celestial Dove,
  Will safely bear me home.

79. *The Christian's Hope.* Auld Lang Syne. **C. M.**

1 Hail, sweetest, dearest tie, that binds
   Our glowing hearts in one;
 Hail, sacred hope, that tunes our minds
   To harmony divine.
 It is the hope, the blissful hope,
   Which Jesus' grace has given —
 The hope, when days and years are past,
   We all shall meet in heaven.

Chorus. We all shall meet in heaven at last,
   We all shall meet in heaven;
 The hope, when days and years are past,
   We all shall meet in heaven.

2 What though the northern, wintry blast
   Shall howl around our cot;
 What though beneath an Eastern sun
   Be cast our distant lot;
 Yet still we share the blissful hope
   Which Jesus' grace has given;
 The hope, when days and years are past,
   We all shall meet in heaven.

3 No lingering look, no parting sigh,
   Our future meeting knows;
 There friendship beams from every eye,
   And love immortal glows.
 O, sacred hope! O, blissful hope!
   Which Jesus' grace has given,
 The hope when days and years are past,
   We all shall meet in heaven.

80. *Indwelling of God desired.* Happy Day. **L. M.**

1 Come, gracious Lord, descend and dwell,
   By faith and love, in every breast;
 Then shall we know, and taste, and feel,
   The joys that cannot be expressed.

2 Come, fill our hearts with inward strength,
   Make our enlargéd souls possess,
 And learn the height, and breadth, and length
   Of thine eternal love and grace.

81. *The Star of Bethlehem.* Bonnie Doon. **L. M.**

1 When, marshalled on the nightly plain,
   The glittering host bestud the sky,
One star alone, of all the train,
   Can fix the sinner's wandering eye.

2 Hark! hark! to God the chorus breaks,
   From every host, from every gem;
But one alone the Saviour speaks,—
   It is the Star of Bethlehem!

3 Once on the raging seas I rode;
   The storm was loud, the night was dark;
The ocean yawned, and rudely blowed
   The wind that tossed my foundering bark.

4 Deep horror then my vitals froze;
   Death-struck, I ceased the tide to stem;
When suddenly a star arose,—
   It was the Star of Bethlehem!

5 It was my guide, my light, my all;
   It bade my dark forebodings cease;
And, through the storm and danger's thrall
   It led me to the port of peace.

6 Now safely moored, my perils o'er,
   I'll sing, first in night's diadem,
Forever, and forevermore,—
   The Star—the Star of Bethlehem!

82. *City of God.* Beautiful Land.

1 A beautiful land by faith I see,
A land of rest, from sorrow free,
The home of the ransomed, bright and fair,
And beautiful angels, too, are there.
    Will you go? Will you go? &c.

2 That beautiful land, the city of light,
It ne'er has known the shades of night;
The glory of God, the light of day,
Hath driven the darkness far away.
    Will you go? Will you go? &c.

83. *The Christian Soldier.* Ortonville. **C. M.**

1 Am I a soldier of the cross,
    A follower of the Lamb?
  And shall I fear to own his cause,
    Or blush to speak his name?

2 Must I be carried to the skies
    On flowery beds of ease,
  While others fought to win the prize,
    And sailed through bloody seas?

3 Are there no foes for me to face?
    Must I not stem the flood?
  Is this vile world a friend to grace,
    To help me on to God?

4 Sure I must fight if I would reign;
    Increase my courage, Lord:
  I'll bear the toil, endure the pain,
    Supported by thy word.

84. *Saints' Home.* I'm going home. **L. M.**

1 My heavenly home is bright and fair;
  Nor pain nor death can enter there;
  Its glittering towers the sun outshine;
  That heavenly mansion shall be mine.

Chorus. I'm going home, I'm going home,
  I'm going home to die no more.
  To die no more, to die no more,
  I'm going home to die no more.

2 My Father's house is built on high,
  Far, far above the starry sky;
  When from this earthly prison free,
  That heavenly mansion mine shall be.

3 Let others seek a home below,
  Which flames devour, or waves o'erflow;
  Be mine the happier lot to own
  A heavenly mansion near the throne.

85. *Weeping Jesus.* Boylston. **S. M.**

1 Did Christ o'er sinners weep,
   And shall our cheeks be dry?
Let floods of penitential grief
   Burst forth from every eye.

2 The Son of God in tears
   Angels with wonder see;
Be thou astonished, O, my soul;
   He shed those tears for thee!

3 He wept that we might weep;
   Each sin demands a tear;
In heaven alone no sin is found,
   And there's no weeping there.

86. *Communion.* Nearer to Thee. **6s & 4s.**

1 Nearer, my God, to thee,
   Nearer to thee!
E'en though it be a cross
   That raiseth me,
Still all my song shall be,
Nearer, my God, to thee,
   Nearer to thee!

2 There let my way appear
   Steps unto heaven;
All that thou sendest me
   In mercy given;
Angels to beckon me
Nearer, my God, to thee,
   Nearer to thee!

3 And when on joyful wing,
   Cleaving the sky,
Sun, moon, and stars forgot,
   Upward I fly,
Still, all my song shall be,
Nearer, my God, to thee,
   Nearer to thee!

87. *Christian Union.* No sorrow there. **L. M.**

1 Come, we that love the Lord,
  And let our joys be known:
Join in a song with sweet accord,
  And thus surround the throne.

2 The sorrows of the mind
  Be banished from the place;
Religion never was designed
  To make our pleasures less.

3 Let those refuse to sing
  That never knew our God;
But favorites of the heavenly King
  May speak their joys abroad.

4 Then let our songs abound,
  And every tear be dry;
We're marching through Immanuel's ground,
  To fairer worlds on high.

88. *Repentance at the Cross of Christ.* **7s & 8s.**

1 Heart of stone, relent, relent;
  Break, by Jesus' cross subdued;
See his body mangled, rent,
  Covered with a gore of blood;
Sinful soul, what hast thou done?
Crucified th' eternal Son.

2 Yes, thy sins have done the deed,
  Driven the nails that fixed him there,
Crowned with thorns his sacred head,
  Plunged into his side the spear,
Made his soul a sacrifice,
While for sinful man he dies.

3 Wilt thou let him bleed in vain?
  Still to death thy Lord pursue?
Open all his wounds again,
  And the shameful cross renew?
No, with all my sins I'll part;
Break, O break, my bleeding heart.

89. *Walking with God.* Balerma. **C. M.**

1 O for a closer walk with God,
   A calm and heavenly frame!
A light to shine upon the road
   That leads me to the Lamb!

2 Where is the blessedness I knew
   When first I saw the Lord?
Where is the soul-refreshing view
   Of Jesus and his word?

3 What peaceful hours I then enjoyed!
   How sweet their memory still!
But now I find an aching void
   The world can never fill.

4 Return, O holy Dove, return,
   Sweet messenger of rest;
I hate the sins that made thee mourn,
   And drove thee from my breast.

90. *Farewell to the World.* **L. M.**

1 Farewell, farewell to all below;
My Jesus calls, and I must go;
I launch my boat upon the sea;
This land is not the land for me.

2 I've found the winding path of sin
A rugged path to travel in;
Beyond the chilly waves I see
The land my Saviour bought for me.

3 Farewell, dear friends; I may not stay;
The home I seek is far away;
Where Christ is not I cannot be;
This land is not the land for me.

4 My hope, my heart, is now on high;
There all my joys and treasures lie;
Where seraphs bow and bend the knee,
O, that's the land, the land for me.

91. *The Land of Rest.* Belford. 7s, 6s, & 8s.

1 Brother, thou art gone to rest;
    We will not weep for thee;
  For thou art now where oft on earth
    Thy spirit longed to be.

2 Brother, thou art gone to rest;
    Thine is an early tomb;
  But Jesus summoned thee away;
    Thy Saviour called thee home.

3 Brother, thou art gone to rest;
    Thy toils and cares are o'er;
  And sorrow, pain, and suffering, now
    Shall ne'er distress thee more.

4 Brother, thou art gone to rest;
    Thy sins are all forgiven,
  And saints in light have welcomed thee
    To share the joys of heaven.

5 Brother, thou art gone to rest;
    And this shall be our prayer,
  That, when we reach our journey's end,
    Thy glory we may share.

92.   *The New Birth.*   C. M.

1 The sovereign will of God alone
    Creates us heirs of grace,
  Born in the image of his Son,
    A new, peculiar race.

2 The Spirit, like some heavenly wind,
    Breathes on the sons of flesh,
  Creates anew the carnal mind,
    And forms the man afresh.

3 Our quickened souls awake and rise
    From their long sleep of death;
  On heavenly things we fix our eyes,
    And praise employs our breath.

93. *I long to go to Heaven.* P. M.

1 O, COME, my loving neighbors, will you go to glory with me?
I long to go to heaven, to my long-sought rest.
O, come, poor mourning sinners, will you go to glory with me?
I long to go to heaven, to my long-sought rest.

Chorus. For the judgment day is rolling round;
Make ready; let us go!

2 O, come, my loving brethren, will you go to glory with me?
I long to go to heaven, to my long-sought rest.
O, come, my loving sisters, will you go to glory with me?
I long to go to heaven, to my long-sought rest.

Chorus. For the judgment day is rolling round;
Make ready; let us go!

94. *God's Army.* Wallace. 7s & 6s.

1 SOLDIERS of the cross, arise!
Lo, your Leader from the skies
Waves before you glory's prize,
  The prize of victory.
Seize your armor — gird it on;
The battle's yours; it will be won;
Though fierce the strife,'t will soon be done;
  Then struggle manfully.

2 Onward, then, ye hosts of God!
Jesus points the victor's rod;
Follow where your Leader trod;
  You soon shall see his face.
Soon, your enemies all slain,
The crown of glory you shall gain,
And walk among that glorious train,
  Who shout their Saviour's praise.

95. *The expiring Saviour.* 8s, 7s, & 4s.

1 Hark! the voice of love and mercy
   Sounds aloud from Calvary:
See! it rends the rocks asunder,
   Shakes the earth, and veils the sky:
     "It is finished!"
Hear the dying Saviour cry.

2 "It is finished!" — O, what pleasure
   Do these charming words afford!
Heavenly blessings without measure
   Flow to us through Christ the Lord:
     "It is finished!"
Saints, the dying words record.

96. *"O, revive us again."* S. M.

1 O Lord, thy work revive
   In Zion's gloomy hour,
And let our dying graces live
   By thy restoring power.

2 O, let thy chosen few
   Awake to earnest prayer,
Their solemn vows again renew,
   And walk in filial fear.

3 Thy Spirit then will speak
   Through lips of humble clay;
O, come, and bring salvation near —
   Our souls on thee rely.

97. *Praise to the Great Jehovah.* Old Hundred. L. M.

1 Be thou, O God, exalted high;
And as thy glory fills the sky,
So let it be on earth displayed,
Till thou art here as there obeyed.

2 O God, my heart is fixed; 'tis bent
Its thankful tribute to present;
And, with my heart, my voice I'll raise
To thee, my God, in songs of praise.

98. *Yet there is Room.* Lenox. H. M.

1 Ye dying sons of men,
  Immerged in sin and woe,
The gospel's voice attend,
  While Jesus sends to you;
Ye perishing and guilty, come;
In Jesus' arms there yet is room.

2 No longer now delay,
  Nor vain excuses frame;
He bids you come to-day,
  Though poor, and blind, and lame:
All things are ready; sinners, come;
For every trembling soul there's room.

99. *Jesus' Invitation.* Expostulation. 8s & 7s.

1 Come, — 'tis Jesus' invitation
  Now to mourning souls addressed;
Why, O, why such hesitation?
  Mourners, he will give you rest.
Chorus. Sinners, can you hate, &c.

2 O, hasten, sinner, to return,
  And stay not for the morrow's sun,
For fear thy lamp should fail to burn
  Before the needful work is done.

100. *Heaven anticipated.* P. M.

1 There is an hour of peaceful rest
  To mourning wanderers given;
There is a joy for souls distressed,
  A balm for every wounded breast;
  'Tis found alone in heaven.

2 There is a home for weary souls,
  By sins and sorrows driven,
When tossed on life's tempestuous shoals,
Where storms arise, and ocean rolls,
  And all is drear — 'tis heaven.

101. *The great Physician.* Morning Light. 7s & 6s.

1 How lost was my condition,
  Till Jesus made me whole!
There is but one Physician
  Can cure a sin-sick soul.
Next door to death he found me,
  And snatched me from the grave;
To tell to all around me
  His wondrous power to save.

2 The worst of all diseases
  Is light, compared with sin;
On every part it seizes,
  But rages most within;
'Tis palsy, plague, and fever,
  And madness, all combined;
And none but a believer
  The least relief can find.

3 From men great skill professing,
  I thought a cure to gain;
But this proved more distressing,
  And added to my pain;
Some said that nothing ailed me,
  Some gave me up for lost;
Thus every refuge failed me,
  And all my hopes were crossed.

4 At length this great Physician —
  How matchless is his grace! —
Accepted my petition,
  And undertook my case;
First gave me sight to view him, —
  For sin my eyes had sealed, —
Then bade me look unto him:
  I looked, and I was healed.

102. *Sweet Prayer.* Sweet Home. **11s.**

1 When torn is the bosom by sorrow or care,
  Be it ever so simple, there's nothing like prayer;
  It eases, soothes, softens, subdues, yet sustains,
  Gives vigor to hope, and puts passion in chains.

Chorus. Prayer, prayer, O, sweet prayer!
  Be it ever so simple, there's nothing like prayer.

2 When far from the friends we hold dearest we part,
  What fond recollections still cling to the heart!
  Past converse, past scenes, past enjoyments are there;
  O, how hurtfully pleasing till hallowed by prayer!

3 When pleasure would woo us from piety's arms,
  The siren sings sweetly, or silently charms,
  We listen, love, loiter, are caught in the snare;
  But looking to Jesus we conquer by prayer.

4 While strangers to prayer we are strangers to bliss;
  Heaven pours its full streams through no channel but this;
  And till we the seraph's full ecstasy share,
  Our chalice of joy must be guarded by prayer.

103. *Great Feast.* Happy Day. **L. M.**

1 Come, sinners, to the gospel feast;
  Let every soul be Jesus' guest;
  Ye need not one be left behind,
  For God hath bidden all mankind.

2 Sent by my Lord, on you I call—
  The invitation is to all!—
  Come, all the world! come, sinner, thou!
  All things in Christ are ready now.

104. *Christ smitten.* Rock of Ages. 7s.

1 Rock of Ages, cleft for me,
Le me hide myself in thee!
Let the water and the blood,
From thy wounded side that flowed,
Be of sin the perfect cure;
Save me, Lord, and make me pure.

2 Should my tears forever flow,
Should my zeal no languor know,—
This for sin could not atone,
Thou must save, and thou alone,
In my hand no price I bring;
Simply to thy cross I cling.

3 While I draw this fleeting breath,
When my eyelids close in death,
When I rise to worlds unknown,
And behold thee on thy throne,
Rock of Ages, cleft for me,
Let me hide myself in thee.

105. *The Mercy-seat.* Bonnie Doon. L. M.

1 From every stormy wind that blows,
From every swelling tide of woes,
There is a calm, a sure retreat;
'Tis found before the mercy-seat.

2 There is a place where Jesus sheds
The oil of gladness on our heads,
A place of all on earth most sweet;
It is the blood-bought mercy-seat.

3 There is a scene where spirits blend,
Where friend holds fellowship with friend;
Though sundered far, by faith they meet
Around one common mercy-seat.

4 There, there, on eagle wings we soar,
And sin and sense molest no more;
And heaven comes down our souls to greet,
And glory crowns the mercy-seat.

106. *Our Home.* Rest for the Weary. 8s & 7s.

1 In the Christian's home in glory
   There remains a land of rest;
   There my Saviour's gone before me,
   To fulfil my soul's request.

Chorus. There is rest for the weary,
   There is rest for you;
   On the other side of Jordan,
   In the sweet fields of Eden,
   Where the tree of life is blooming,
   There is rest for you.

2 He is fitting up a mansion,
   Which eternally shall stand;
   For my stay shall not be transient
   In that holy, happy land.

3 Pain and sickness ne'er shall enter,
   Grief nor woe my lot shall share;
   But in that celestial centre
   I a crown of life shall wear.

107. *Admonition.* Robert Kidd. 12s.

1 Remember, sinful youth, you must die! you must die!
Remember, sinful youth, you must die!
Remember, sinful youth, who hate the way of [truth,
And in your pleasures boast, you must die! you must die!
And in your pleasures boast, you must die.

2 And if you travel down the broad road, the broad road,
And if you travel down the broad road,
And if you travel down, to darkness you are bound,
Eternally around, the broad road, &c.

3 To a dreadful judgment day you are bound, you are bound,
To a dreadful judgment day you are bound,
To a dreadful judgment day, be your thoughts whate'er they may;
Nor can you it delay, you are bound, &c.

108. *Christ's Advent.* Old Bay State. **P. M.**

1 You will see your Lord a coming, you will see
  your Lord a coming,
 You will see your Lord a coming, from the old
  church yards,
 While the band of music, while the band of
  music,
 While the band of music shall be sounding
  through the air.

2 There will be a mighty wailing, &c.

3 Then, O sinner, you will tremble, &c.

4 You will flee to rocks and mountains, &c.

5 You will see the saints arising, &c.

6 Angels bear them to the Saviour, &c.

109. *Call to the Unconverted.* **8s & 4s.**

1 HARK! hark! the gospel trumpet sounds;
 Through earth and heaven the echo bounds;
 Pardon and peace by Jesus' blood!
 Sinners are reconciled to God,
 Sinners are reconciled to God,
  By grace divine.

2 Come, sinners, hear the joyful news;
 No longer dare the grace refuse;
 Mercy and justice here combine;
 Goodness and truth harmonious join,
 Goodness and truth harmonious join,
  T' invite you near.

3 Ye saints in glory, strike the lyre;
 Ye mortals, catch the sacred fire;
 Let both the Saviour's love proclaim,
 Forever worthy is the Lamb,
 Forever worthy is the Lamb,
  Of endless praise.

110. *Land of Rest.* C. M.

1 O, LAND of rest, for thee I sigh;
  When will the moment come
 When I shall lay my armor by,
  And dwell with Christ at home?

2 No tranquil joys on earth I know;
  No peaceful, sheltering dome;
 This world's a wilderness of woe;
  This world is not my home.

3 To Jesus Christ I sought for rest;
  He bade me cease to roam,
 And fly for succor to his breast,
  And he'd conduct me home.

4 I would at once have quit the place,
  Where foes and fury roam;
 But, ah! my passport was not sealed;
  I could not yet go home.

5 When, by afflictions sharply tried,
  I viewed the gaping tomb,
 Although I dread death's chilling flood,
  Yet still I sighed for home.

6 Weary of wandering round and round
  This vale of sin and gloom,
 I long to leave th' unhallowed ground,
  And dwell with Christ at home.

111. *Decision.* The Sinner's Resolve. C. M.

1 COME, trembling sinner, in whose breast
  A thousand thoughts revolve;
 Come, with your guilt and fear oppressed,
  And make this last resolve:—

2 I'll go to Jesus, though my sin
  Hath like a mountain rose;
 I know his courts, I'll enter in,
  Whatever may oppose.

112. *Heavenly Union.* L. M. 8s.

1 ATTEND, ye saints, and hear me tell
The wonders of Immanuel,
Who saved me from a burning hell,
And brought my soul with him to dwell,
  And gave me heavenly union.

2 When Jesus saw me from on high,
Beheld my soul in ruin lie,
He looked on me with pitying eye,
And said to me, as he passed by,
  "With God you have no union."

3 Then I began to weep and cry,
And looked this way and that to fly;
It grieved me sore that I must die;
I strove salvation for to buy;
  But still I had no union!

4 But when I hated all my sin,
My dear Redeemer took me in,
And with his blood he washed me clean;
And O, what seasons I have seen,
  Since first I felt this union!

5 I praised the Lord both night and day,
And went from house to house to pray,
And if I met one on the way,
I found I'd something still to say
  About this heavenly union.

6 I now with saints can join to sing,
And mount on faith's triumphant wing,
And make the heavenly arches ring
With loud hosannas to our King,
  Who brought our souls to union.

7 Sing to the Lord a noble song!
Awake, my soul — awake, my tongue;
Hosanna to th' eternal name,
And all his boundless love proclaim,
  For grace and heavenly union.

113. *The emblematic Dove.* — *Baptism.* **C. M.**

1 Meekly in Jordan's holy stream
  The great Redeemer bowed;
Bright was the glory's sacred beam
  That hushed the wondering crowd.

2 Thus God descended to approve
  The deed that Christ had done;
Thus came the emblematic Dove,
  And hovered o'er the Son.

3 So, blessèd Spirit, come to-day
  To our baptismal scene;
Let thoughts of earth be far away,
  And every mind serene.

4 This day we give to holy joy;
  This day to heaven belongs;
Raised to new life, we will employ
  In melody our tongues.

114. *Meeting.* Say, Brothers. **C. M.**

1 Say, brothers, will you meet us,
  Say, brothers, will you meet us,
  Say, brothers, will you meet us,
    On Canaan's happy shore?

Chorus. By the grace of God we'll meet you,
  By the grace of God we'll meet you,
  By the grace of God we'll meet you,
    Where parting is no more.

2 Jesus lives and reigns forever,
  Jesus lives and reigns forever,
  Jesus lives and reigns forever,
    On Canaan's happy shore.

  Glory, glory, hallelujah;
  Glory, glory, hallelujah;
  Glory, glory, hallelujah,
    Forever, evermore.

115. *Prayer for a Revival.* Good Shepherd. 8s, 7s, 4s.

1 Saviour, visit thy plantation;
    Grant us, Lord, a gracious rain;
  All will come to desolation
    Unless thou return again.
      Lord, revive us!
    All our help must come from thee.

2 Surely once thy garden flourished;
    Every part looked gay and green;
  All its plants by thee were nourished;
    Then how cheering was the scene!
      Lord, revive us!
    All our help must come from thee.

3 Keep no longer at a distance;
    Shine upon us from on high,
  Lest, for want of thine assistance
    Every plant should droop and die.
      Lord, revive us!
    All our help must come from thee.

4 Dearest Saviour, hasten hither;
    Thou canst make them bloom again;
  O, permit them not to wither;
    Let not all our hopes be vain.
      Lord, revive us!
    All our help must come from thee.

5 Let our mutual love be fervent;
    Make us prevalent in prayers;
  Let each one esteemed thy servant
    Shun the world's bewitching snares.
      Lord, revive us!
    All our help must come from thee.

6 Break the tempter's fatal power,
    Turn the stony heart to flesh,
  And begin, from this good hour,
    To revive thy work afresh.
      Lord, revive us!
    All our help must come from thee.

116. *Jesus' Reign.* **P. M.**

1 Hear the royal proclamation,
  Joyful tidings of salvation,
  Publishing to every creature,
  To the ruined sons of nature,

Chorus. Jesus reigns — he reigns victorious;
  Over heaven and earth most glorious,
  Jesus reigns.

2 See the royal banners flying!
  Hear the herald loudly crying!
  Rebel sinners, royal favor
  Now is offered by the Saviour.
           Lo, he reigns, &c.

3 Hear, ye sons of wrath and ruin,
  Who have wrought your own undoing:
  Here is life and free salvation
  Offered to the whole creation.
           Jesus reigns, &c.

4 'Twas for you that Jesus died,
  For you your Lord was crucified,
  Conquered death, and rose to heaven,
  Life eternal through him given.
           Lo, he reigns, &c.

5 Turn unto the Lord most holy,
  Shun the paths of vice and folly —
  Roaring thunders, lightning's blazes,
  Shout the great Messiah's praises.
           Jesus reigns, &c.

6 Shout, ye tongues of every nation,
  To the bounds of the creation;
  Shout the praise of Judah's Lion,
  The Almighty Prince of Zion.
           Jesus reigns, &c.

117. *Lord, remember me.* Pisgah. **C. M.**

1 Jesus, thou art the sinner's friend;
  As such I look to thee;
 Now, in the bowels of thy love,
  O Lord, remember me.

2 Remember thy pure word of grace:
  Remember Calvary;
 Remember all thy dying groans,
  And then remember me.

3 Thou wondrous Advocate with God!
  I yield myself to thee;
 While thou art sitting on thy throne,
  O Lord, remember me.

4 I own I'm guilty, own I'm vile;
  Yet thy salvation's free:
 Then, in thy all-abounding grace,
  O Lord, remember me.

5 Howe'er forsaken or distressed,
  Howe'er oppressed I be,
 Howe'er afflicted here on earth,
  Do thou remember me.

6 And when I close my eyes in death,
  And creature helps all flee,
 Then, O my great Redeemer, God,
  I pray, remember me.

118. *Parting.* **L. M.**

1 Farewell, dear friends; I must be gone;
  I have no home or stay with you;
 I'll take my staff and travel on,
  Till I a better world do view.

Chorus. Farewell, farewell, farewell,
  My loving friends, farewell.

2 Farewell, young converts of the cross;
  O, labor hard for Christ and heaven;
 You've counted all things here but dross;
  Fight on; the crown will soon be given.

119. *The Jubilee proclaimed.* Lenox. **H. M.**

1 Blow ye the trumpet, blow,
 The gladly-solemn sound;
Let all the nations know,
 To earth's remotest bound,
The year of jubilee is come;
Return, ye ransomed sinners, home.

2 Exalt the Lamb of God,
 The sin-atoning Lamb;
Redemption by his blood
 Through all the lands proclaim.
The year of jubilee is come;
Return, ye ransomed sinners, home.

3 The gospel trumpet hear,
 The news of pardoning grace;
Ye happy souls, draw near;
 Behold your Saviour's face;
The year of jubilee is come;
Return, ye ransomed sinners, home.

4 Jesus, our great High Priest,
 Has full atonement made;
Ye weary spirits, rest;
 Ye mourning souls, be glad:
The year of jubilee is come,
Return, ye ransomed sinners, home.

Emancipation.   8s & 7s.

When I was down in Egypt land;
 I want to wear the crown.
I heard tell of the promised land;
 I want to wear the crown.
  My heart says, praise the Lord, &c.

My dungeon shook, my chains fell off;
 I want to wear the crown.
Glory to God my soul did cry;
 I want to wear the crown.
  My heart says, praise the Lord, &c.

121. *Revival Blessings.* C. P. M.

1 The Lord into his garden comes;
The spices yield their rich perfumes;
 The lilies grow and thrive;
Refreshing showers of grace divine
From Jesus flow to every vine,
 And make the dead revive.

2 This makes the dry and barren ground
In springs of water to abound,
 And fruitful soil become;
The desert blossoms like the rose,
When Jesus conquers all his foes,
 And makes his people one.

3 The glorious time is rolling on,
The gracious work is now begun;
 My soul a witness is;
Come, taste and see the pardon free
To all mankind as well as me;
 Who come to Christ may live.

4 The worst of sinners here may find
A Saviour pitiful and kind,
 Who will them all relieve:
None are too late if they repent;
Out of one sinner legions went;
 Jesus did him receive.

122. *Zion waking.* Pilgrim. 8s & 7s.

1 Met, O God, to ask thy presence,
 Join our hearts to seek thy grace;
O, deny us not, nor spurn us;
 Let us see thy smiling face.

Chorus. We are bound for the kingdom, &c.

2 We have wandered, long have wandered,
 Much deserve thy chastening rod;
But we come to own our folly;
 Heal and pardon, O, our God.

123.   *The Way-faring Man.*   **L. M. D.**

1 A poor, wayfaring man of grief
    Hath often crossed me on my way,
Who sued so humbly for relief,
    That I could never answer nay;
I had not power to ask his name,
Whither he went or whence he came;
Yet there was something in his eye
That won my love, I knew not why.

2 Once, when my scanty meal was spread,
    He entered; not a word he spake;
Just perishing for want of bread,
    I gave him all; he blessed it, brake,
And ate, but gave me part again;
Mine was an angel's portion then,
And while I fed with eager haste,
The crust was manna to my taste.

3 I spied him where a fountain burst
    Clear from the rock; his strength was gone;
The heedless water mocked his thirst;
    He heard it, saw it hurrying on.
I ran and raised the sufferer up;
Thrice from the stream he drained my cup,
Dipped and returned it running o'er;
I drank, and never thirsted more.

4 Then, in a moment, to my view,
    The stranger started from disguise;
The tokens in his hands I knew;
    My Saviour stood before my eyes.
He spake, and my poor name he named:—
"Of me thou hast not been ashamed;
These deeds shall thy memorial be;
Fear not; thou didst it unto me."

124.   *Something new.*   **C. M.**

1 Since man by sin has lost his God,
    He seeks creation through,
  And vainly strives for solid bliss
    In trying something new.

2 The new possessed, like fading flowers,
    Soon loses its gay hue;
  The bubble now no longer charms;
    The mind wants something new.

3 Could we but call all Europe ours,
    With India and Peru,
  The mind would feel an aching void,
    And still want something new.

4 But when the Saviour's love we feel,
    All good in him we view;
  The mind forsakes its vain delights,
    In Christ finds something new.

5 The joys the dear Redeemer gives
    Will bear a strict review;
  Nor need we ever change again,
    For Christ is always new.

6 Cheerful we'll walk the road to bliss,
    Joined with a happy few;
  And when we reach our journey's end,
    Find heaven forever new.

125.   *Christ our Guide.*   Salvation.   **L. M.**

1 Jesus, my truth, my way,
    My sure, unerring light,
  On thee my feeble soul I stay,
    Which thou wilt lead aright.

2 My wisdom and my guide,
    My counsellor, thou art;
  O, never let me leave thy side,
    Or from thy paths depart.

126. *Our Country.* America. **6s & 4s.**

1 My country, 'tis of thee,
  Sweet land of liberty,
    Of thee I sing;
  Land where my fathers died,
  Land of the pilgrims' pride,
  From every mountain side,
    Let freedom ring!

2 My native country, thee —
  Land of the noble, free —
    Thy name I love:
  I love thy rocks and rills,
  Thy woods and templed hills;
  My heart with rapture thrills
    Like that above.

3 Let music swell the breeze,
  And ring from all the trees
    Sweet freedom's song!
  Let mortal tongues awake;
  Let all that breathe partake;
  Let rocks their silence break, —
    The sound prolong!

4 Our fathers' God, to thee,
  Author of liberty,
    To thee we sing:
  Long may our land be bright
  With freedom's holy light;
  Protect us by thy might,
    Great God, our King.

127. *Doxology.* **8s, 7s, & 4s.**

1 Great Jehovah, we adore thee,
    God the Father, God the Son,
  God the Spirit, joined in glory
    On the same eternal throne:
      Endless praises
    To Jehovah, three in one.

128. *Invitation.* Just now. 8s & 6s.

1 Come to Jesus, come to Jesus,
  Come to Jesus just now;
 Just now, come to Jesus,
  Come to Jesus, just now.

2 He will save you, he will save you, &c.
3 Don't reject him, don't reject him, &c.
4 Only trust him, only trust him, &c.
5 He is willing, just now, &c.
6 He is able, just now, &c.
7 He is knocking, just now, &c.
8 Time is flying, just now, &c.
9 Will you linger, just now, &c.
10 Come, poor sinner, just now, &c.
11 Christ is pleading, just now, &c.
12 Do not slight him, just now, &c.
13 God is waiting, just now, &c.
14 Christ may leave you, just now, &c.
15 Love the Saviour, just now, &c.
16 Pray on, brethren, just now, &c.
17 Pray on, sisters, just now, &c.
18 Satan trembles, just now, &c.
19 Heaven rejoices, just now, &c.

129. *Captivity led captive.* H. M.

1 THE happy morn is come:
  Triumphant o'er the grave,
 The Saviour leaves the tomb,
  Omnipotent to save:
 Captivity is captive led;
 For Jesus liveth, that was dead.

2 Christ hath the ransom paid;
  The glorious work is done;
 On him our help is laid,
  By him our victory won:
 Captivity is captive led;
 For Jesus liveth, that was dead.

130. *Source of Blessings.* Nettleton. 8s & 7s.

1 Holy Source of consolation,
  Light and life thy grace imparts;
 Visit us in thy compassion;
  Guide our minds, and fill our hearts.

2 Heavenly blessings, without measure,
  Thou canst bring us from above;
 Lord, we ask that heavenly treasure,
  Wisdom, holiness, and love.

3 Dwell within us, bless*é*d Spirit;
  Where thou art no ill can come;
 Bless us now through Jesus' merit;
  Reign in every heart and home.

4 Saviour, lead us to adore thee,
  While thou dost prolong our days;
 Then, with angel hosts before thee,
  May we worship, love, and praise.

131. *Sovereign Grace.* Grace. 7s.

1 Sovereign grace has power alone
 To subdue a heart of stone;
 And the moment grace is felt,
 Then the hardest heart will melt.

2 When the Lord was crucified,
 Two transgressors with him died;
 One, with vile blaspheming tongue,
 Scoffed at Jesus as he hung.

3 But the other, touched with grace,
 Saw the danger of his case;
 Faith received to own the Lord,
 Whom the scribes and priests abhorred.

4 This was wondrous grace indeed,
 Grace bestowed in time of need;
 Sinners, trust in Jesus' name;
 You shall find him still the same.

132. *Assurance.* Canaan. **L. M.**

1 I'm glad that I was born to die;
  I am bound for the land of Canaan;
From grief and woe my soul shall fly;
  I am bound for the land of Canaan;

2 Bright angels shall convey me home,
  Away to New Jerusalem.

3 I have some friends before me gone,
  And I'm resolved to follow on;

4 They're happy round my Father's throne;
  They're looking out for me to come.

5 I hope to meet my brethren there,
  Who used to join with me in prayer;

6 If you get there before I do,
  Look out for me; I'm coming too.

7 I'll praise my Maker while I've breath;
  I hope to praise him after death;

8 I hope to praise him when I die,
  And shout salvation as I fly.

133. *Encouragement to Faithfulness.* No Sorrow. **S. M.**

1 Our Captain leads us on;
  He beckons from the skies;
He reaches out a starry crown,
  And bids us take the prize.

2 "Be faithful unto death,
  Partake my victory,
And thou shalt wear this glorious wreath,
  And thou shalt reign with me."

3 Who conquer in his might
  The victor's meed receive;
They claim a kingdom in his right,
  Which God will freely give.

134. *Christ precious to Believers.* I do believe. **C. M.**

1 How sweet the name of Jesus sounds
 In a believer's ear!
It soothes his sorrows, heals his wounds,
 And drives away his fear.

2 It makes the wounded spirit whole,
 And calms the troubled breast;
'Tis manna to the hungry soul,
 And to the weary rest.

3 Dear name! the rock on which I build,
 My shield and hiding-place,
My never-failing treasury, filled
 With boundless stores of grace.

4 So, then, I would thy love proclaim
 With every fleeting breath;
And may the music of thy name
 Refresh my soul in death.

135. *Gratitude.* Ortonville. **C. M.**

1 When all thy mercies, O my God,
 My rising soul surveys,
Transported with the view, I'm lost
 In wonder, love, and praise.

2 Unnumbered comforts on my soul
 Thy tender care bestowed,
Before my infant heart conceived
 From whom those comforts flowed.

3 When in the slippery paths of youth
 With heedless steps I ran,
Thine arm, unseen, conveyed me safe,
 And led me up to man.

4 Through every period of my life,
 Thy goodness I'll pursue,
And after death, in distant worlds,
 The glorious theme renew.

136. *Delight.* I want to be an Angel. 6s & 7s.

1 I WANT to be an angel,
 And with the angels stand,
A crown upon my forehead,
 A harp within my hand;
There, right before my Saviour,
 So glorious and so bright,
I'd wake the sweetest music,
 And praise him day and night.

2 I never should be weary,
 Nor ever shed a tear,
Nor ever know a sorrow,
 Nor ever feel a fear;
But blessèd, pure, and holy,
 I'd dwell in Jesus' sight,
And, with ten thousand thousand,
 I'd praise him day and night.

3 I know I'm weak and sinful,
 But Jesus will forgive;
For many little children
 Have gone to heaven to live;
Dear Saviour, when I languish,
 And lay me down to die,
O, send a shining angel
 To bear me to the sky.

4 O, there I'll be an angel,
 And with the angels stand,
A crown upon my forehead,
 A harp within my hand;
And there, before my Saviour,
 So glorious and so bright,
I'll join the heavenly music,
 And praise him day and night.

137. *Glorying in the Cross.* Pleading. 8s & 7s. D.

1 In the cross of Christ I glory,
    Towering o'er the wrecks of time;
All the light of sacred story
    Gathers round its head sublime.
        Chorus. Turn to the Lord, &c.

2 When the waves of life o'ertake me,
    Hopes deceive and fears annoy,
Never shall the cross forsake me;
    Lo! it glows with peace and joy.

3 When the sun of bliss is beaming
    Light and love upon my way,
From the cross the radiance streaming
    Adds new lustre to the day.

4 Grief and blessing, pain and pleasure,
    By the cross are sanctified;
Peace is there that knows no measure,
    Joys that through all time abide.

5 In the cross of Christ I glory,
    Towering o'er the wrecks of time;
All the light of sacred story
    Gathers round its head sublime.

138. *Holy Jerusalem.* C. M.

1 Jerusalem, my happy home,
    O, how I long for thee!
When will my sorrows have an end?
    Thy joys when shall I see?

2 Jesus, my Lord, to glory's gone;
    Him will I go and see;
And all my brethren here below
    Will soon come after me.

3 When we've been there ten thousand years,
    Bright shining as the sun,
We've no less days to sing God's praise
    Than when we first begun.

139. *Christ the Way.* Happy Day. **L. M.**

1 Jesus, my all, to heaven is gone —
He whom I fix my hopes upon;
His track I see, and I'll pursue
The narrow way, till him I view.
Chorus. Happy day, happy day, &c.

2 The way the holy prophets went,
The road that leads from banishment,
The king's highway of holiness —
I'll go, for all his paths are peace.
Happy day, happy day, &c.

3 This is the way I long have sought,
And mourned because I found it not;
My grief and burden long have been
Because I could not cease from sin.
Happy day, happy day, &c.

4 The more I strove against its power,
I sinned and stumbled but the more;
Till late I heard my Saviour say,
"Come hither, soul; I am the way."
Happy day, happy day, &c.

5 Lo! glad I come; and thou, blest Lamb,
Shalt take me to thee as I am;
My sinful self to thee I give;
Nothing but love shall I receive.
Happy day, happy day, &c.

140. *The Great Commission.* **L. M.**

1 "Go, teach the nations, and baptize,"
Aloud th' ascending Jesus cries;
His glad apostles took the word,
And through the nations preached their Lord.

2 Lord, in thy house they seek thy face;
O, bless them with peculiar grace!
Refresh their souls with love divine;
Let beams of glory round them shine.

141. *Bartimeus.* 8s & 7s.

1 Mercy, O thou son of David!
  Thus poor blind Bartimeus prayed!
Others by thy grace are saved;
  Now vouchsafe to me thy aid.
For his crying many chid him;
  But he prayed the louder still,
Till his gracious Saviour bid him,
  Come and ask me what you will.

2 Money was not what he wanted,
  Though by begging used to live;
But he asked and Jesus granted
  Alms which none but he could give:
Lord, remove this grievous blindness,
  Let mine eyes behold the day:
Straight he saw, and won by kindness,
  Followed Jesus in the way.

3 Now methinks I hear him singing,
  Publishing to all around:
Friends, is not my case amazing?
  What a Saviour I have found!
O that all the blind but knew him,
  And would be advised by me,
Sure if they would come unto him,
  He would cause them all to see.

142. *Heavenly Home.* P. M.

1 My heavenly home is bright and fair;
  I have a home in glory;
Nor pain nor death can enter there;
  I have a home in glory.
    Chorus. O, glory! O, glory, &c.

2 Its glittering towers the sun outshine;
  I have a home in glory;
That heavenly mansion shall be mine;
  I have a home in glory.
      O, glory! O, glory, &c.

143. *The Crisis.* Ganges. 8s & 6s.

1 Lo! on a narrow neck of land,
 'Twixt two unbounded seas, I stand,
  Yet how insensible!
 A point of time, a moment's space,
 Removes me to yon heavenly place,
  Or shuts me up in hell.

2 O God, my inmost soul convert,
 And deeply on my thoughtful heart
  Eternal things impress;
 Give me to feel their solemn weight,
 And save me, ere it be too late,
  By free and sovereign grace.

144. *Prayer.* Ortonville. C. M.

1 PRAYER is the soul's sincere desire,
  Unuttered or expressed,
 The motion of a hidden fire,
  That trembles in the breast.

2 Prayer is the simplest form of speech
  That infant lips can try;
 Prayer, the sublimest strains that reach
  The majesty on high.

3 Prayer is the Christian's vital breath,
  The Christian's native air,
 His watchword at the gates of death;
  He enters heaven with prayer.

145. *Farewell.* Old Hundred. L. M.

1 COME, Christian brethren, ere we part,
 Join every voice and every heart;
 One solemn hymn to God we'll raise,
 One final song of grateful praise.

2 Christians, we here may meet no more,
 But there is yet a happier shore;
 And there, released from toil and pain,
 Dear brethren, we shall meet again.

146. *Bible leads to Glory.*

1 My Bible leads to glory,
My Bible leads to glory,
My Bible leads to glory,
Ye followers of the Lamb.

Chorus. Sing on, pray on, ye followers of Immanuel,
Sing on, pray on, ye followers of the Lamb.

2 Religion makes me happy, &c.
Ye followers of the Lamb, &c.

3 I'm on my way to glory, &c.
Ye followers of the Lamb, &c.

4 I'm fighting for a kingdom, &c.
Ye followers of the Lamb, &c.

5 King Jesus is my captain, &c.
Ye followers of the Lamb, &c.

6 We'll have a shout in glory, &c.
Ye followers of the Lamb, &c.

7 There we shall live forever, &c.
Ye followers of the Lamb, &c.

147. *The Dying Christian.* Bower of Prayer. **11s.**

1 My soul's full of glory, inspiring my tongue;
Could I meet with angels, I'd sing them a song;
I'd sing of my Jesus, and tell of his charms,
And beg them to bear me to his loving arms.

2 Sweet Spirit, attend me, till Jesus shall come,
Protect and defend me until I'm called home;
Though worms my poor body may claim as their prey,
'Twill outshine, when rising, the sun at noonday.

3 Farewell, my dear brethren, my Lord bids me come;
Farewell, my dear sisters; I'm now going home;
Bright angels are whispering so sweet in my ear!
Away to my Saviour my spirit they'll bear.

148. *Benevolence.* 7s & 8s.

1 My brother, I wish you well,
 My brother, I wish you well,
 When my Lord calls, I trust I shall
 Be mentioned in the promised land.
Chorus. Be mentioned in the promised land,
 Be mentioned in the promised land;
 When my Lord calls, I trust I shall
 Be mentioned in the promised land.

2 My sister, I wish you well, &c.
3 My father, I wish you well, &c.
4 My mother, I wish you well, &c.
5 My neighbors, I wish you well, &c.
6 My pastor, I wish you well, &c.
7 Young converts, I wish you well, &c.
8 Poor sinners, I wish you well, &c.

149. *Christians buried and risen with Christ.* C. M.

1 Baptized into our Saviour's death,
 Our souls to sin must die;
 With Christ our Lord we live anew,
 With Christ ascend on high.

2 There, by his Father's side he sits,
 Enthroned divinely fair,
 Yet owns himself our Brother still,
 And our Forerunner there.

3 Rise from these earthly trifles, rise,
 On wings of faith and love;
 Above our choicest treasure lies,—
 And be our hearts above.

4 But earth and sin will draw us down,
 When we attempt to fly;
 Lord, send thy strong, attractive power
 To fix our souls on high.

150. *The Cross.* Cleansing Fountain. **C. M.**

1 Must Jesus bear the cross alone,
  And all the world go free?
No: there's a cross for every one,
  And there's a cross for me.
  And there's a cross for me.
  And there's a cross for me.
No: there's a cross for every one,
  And there's a cross for me.

2 How faithful does the Saviour prove
  To those who serve him here!
They now may taste his precious love,
  And joy to hail him near,
  And joy to hail him near, &c.

3 We'll bear the consecrated cross,
  Till from the cross set free,
And then go home to wear the crown:
  O, there's a crown for me,
  O, there's a crown for me, &c

4 O, precious cross! O, glorious crown!
  O, resurrection day!
Ye angels from the stars come down,
  And bear my soul away,
  And bear my soul away, &c.

151. *Pray, pray, pray.* Loving-kindness. **L. M.**

1 Pray on, my brethren in the Lord;
Pray till you feel the power of God;
Pray till he drives your doubts away;
Pray till you see the gospel day.
  Chorus. His loving-kindness, loving-kindness,
    His loving-kindness, O, how free!

2 Soon you shall have your hearts' desire;
Our God will answer us by fire;
You'll see the effect of fervent prayer
In the abundant grace you share.

152. *Longing Flock.* Nettleton. 8s & 7s.

1 Let thy kingdom, blessèd Saviour,
  Come, and bid our jarring cease;
Come, O, come, and reign forever,
  God of love and Prince of peace.
Visit now poor bleeding Zion,
  Hear thy people mourn and weep;
Day and night thy lambs are crying:
  Come, good Shepherd, feed thy sheep.

2 Some for Paul, some for Apollos,
  Some for Cephas — none agree;
Jesus, let us hear thee call us;
  Help us, Lord, to follow thee.
Then we'll rush through what encumbers,
  Over every hinderance leap,
Not upheld by force or numbers;
  Come, good Shepherd, feed thy sheep.

3 Lord, in us there is no merit;
  We've been sinners from our youth;
Guide us, Lord, by thy good Spirit,
  Which shall teach us all the truth.
On thy gospel word we'll venture,
  Till in death's cold arms we sleep,
Love our Lord, and Christ our Saviour:
  O, good Shepherd, feed thy sheep.

4 Christ alone, whose merit saves us,
  Taught by him, we'll own his name;
Sweetest of all names is Jesus;
  How it doth our souls inflame!
Glory, glory, glory, glory,
  Give him glory: he will keep;
He will clear our way before us:
  The good Shepherd feeds his sheep.

153.   *Come, thou Fount.*   Greenville.   8s & 7s.

1 Come, thou fount of every blessing,
    Tune my heart to sing thy grace;
  Streams of mercy never ceasing
    Call for songs of loudest praise.
  Teach me some melodious sonnet,
    Sung by flaming tongues above;
  Praise the mount — I'm fixed upon it,
    Mount of God's unchanging love.

2 Here I'll raise my Ebenezer;
    Hither by thy help I'm come;
  And I hope, by thy good pleasure,
    Safely to arrive at home.
  Jesus sought me when a stranger,
    Wandering from the fold of God;
  He, to save my soul from danger,
    Interposed his precious blood.

3 O, to grace how great a debtor
    Daily I'm constrained to be!
  Let that grace, Lord, like a fetter,
    Bind my wandering heart to thee!
  Prone to wander, Lord, I feel it,
    Prone to leave the God I love:
  Here's my heart; O, take and seal it;
    Seal it from thy courts above.

154.   *Faithful.*   6s, 10s, & 7s.

1 I'll try to prove faithful,
  I'll try to prove faithful,
  I'll try to prove faithful, faithful, faithful,
  Till we all shall meet above.

2 O, let us prove faithful, &c.
3 We mean to be faithful, &c.
4 There'll be no more sinning, &c.
  When we all shall meet above.
5 There'll be no more sorrow, &c.
6 There we shall see Jesus, &c.
7 There we shall sing praises, &c.

155.   *Christian Union.*   De Fleury. 8s.

1 From whence doth this union arise,
    That hatred is conquered by love?
  It fastens our souls in such ties
    As distance and time can't remove.

2 It cannot in Eden be found,
    Nor yet in a Paradise lost;
  It grows on Immanuel's ground,
    And Jesus' dear blood it did cost.

3 My friends are so dear unto me,
    Our hearts all united in love!
  Where Jesus has gone we shall be—
    In yonder bright mansions above.

4 O, why, then, so loath now to part,
    Since we shall ere long meet again?
  Engraved on Immanuel's heart,
    At distance we cannot remain.

5 And when we shall see that bright day,
    And join with the angels above,
  And, leaving these bodies of clay,
    Unite with our Jesus in love,—

6 With Jesus we ever shall reign;
    We all his bright glory shall see,
  And sing, "Hallelujah, Amen:"
    Amen, even so let it be.

156.   *Prayer.*   C. M.

1 Prayer is the contrite sinner's voice
    Returning from his ways,
  While angels in their songs rejoice,
    And cry, "Behold, he prays."

2 The saints in prayer appear as one,
    In word, and deed, and mind,
  While with the Father and the Son
    Sweet fellowship they find.

157. *The Road to Life and to Death.* Windham. **L.M.**

1 Broad is the road that leads to death,
   And thousands walk together there;
But wisdom shows a narrow path,
   With here and there a traveller.

2 "Deny thyself, and take thy cross,"
   Is the Redeemer's great command;
Nature must count her gold but dross,
   If she would gain this heavenly land.

3 The fearful soul that tires and faints,
   And walks the ways of God no more,
Is but esteemed almost a saint,
   And makes his own destruction sure.

4 Lord, let not all my hopes be vain;
   Create my heart entirely new;
Which hypocrites could ne'er attain,
   Which false apostates never knew.

158. *Glorious Hope.* **C.M.**

1 I know that my Redeemer lives,
   And ever prays for me;
A token of his love he gives,
   A pledge of liberty.

2 I find him lifting up my head;
   He brings salvation near;
His presence makes me free indeed,
   And he will soon appear.

3 Jesus, I hang upon thy word;
   I steadfastly believe
Thou wilt return, and claim me, Lord,
   And to thyself receive.

4 Joyful in hope, my spirit soars
   To meet thee from above,
Thy goodness thankfully adores;
   And sure I taste thy love.

159. *The Sanctifier.* Ice and Snow. 7s.

1 Holy Ghost, with light divine,
Shine upon this heart of mine;
Chase the shades of night away;
Turn the darkness into day.

2 Holy Ghost, with power divine,
Cleanse this guilty heart of mine;
Long has sin, without control,
Held dominion o'er my soul.

3 Holy Ghost, with joy divine,
Cheer this saddened heart of mine;
Bid my many woes depart;
Heal my wounded, bleeding heart.

4 Holy Spirit, all divine,
Dwell within this heart of mine;
Cast down every idol throne;
Reign supreme, and reign alone.

160. *Christ crucified.* Penitence. 7s, 6s, & 8s.

1 Vain, delusive world, adieu,
  With all of creature good;
Only Jesus I pursue,
  Who bought me with his blood;
All thy pleasures I forego,
  I trample on thy wealth and pride:
    Only Jesus will I know,
    And Jesus crucified.

2 Him to know is life and peace,
  And pleasure without end;
This is all my happiness —
  On Jesus to depend,
Daily in his grace to grow,
  And ever in his faith abide:
    Only Jesus will I know,
    And Jesus crucified.

161. *Fountain.* Garden. **C. P. M.**

1 Come, brethren, you that love the Lord,
Who taste the sweetness of his word,
　In Jesus' ways go on;
Our troubles and our trials here,
Will only make us richer there,
　When we arrive at home.

2 We feel that heaven is now begun;
It issues from the shining throne,
　From Jesus' throne on high;
It comes like floods; we can't contain;
We drink, and drink, and drink again,
　And yet we still are dry.

3 But when we come to reign above,
And all surround the throne of love,
　We'll drink a full supply;
Jesus will lead his armies through
To living fountains where they flow,
　That never will run dry.

4 There we shall reign, and shout and sing,
And make the upper regions ring,
　When all the saints get home;
Come on, come on, my brethren dear;
Soon we shall meet together there,
　For Jesus bids us come.

162. *Supporting Grace.* **C. M.**

1 How happy is the Christian's state!
　His sins are all forgiven;
A cheering ray confirms the grace,
　And lifts his hopes to heaven.

2 Though, in the rugged path of life,
　He heaves the pensive sigh,
Yet, trusting in the Lord, he finds
　Supporting grace is nigh.

163. *Our Joy in Hope.* Ice and Snow. 7s.

1 Children of the heavenly King,
  As ye journey, sweetly sing;
Sing your Saviour's worthy praise,
  Glorious in his works and ways.

2 We are travelling home to God
  In the way the fathers trod;
They are happy now, and we
  Soon their happiness shall see.

3 Shout, ye little flock, and blest;
  You near Jesus' throne shall rest;
There your seats are now prepared,
  There your kingdom and reward.

4 Fear not, brethren; joyful stand
  On the borders of your land:
Jesus Christ, your Father's Son,
  Bids you undismayed go on.

164. *Remembrance.* Auld Lang Syne.

1 Jesus, thy love shall we forget,
  And never bring to mind
The grace that paid our hopeless debt,
  And bade us pardon find?

Chorus. Our sorrows and our sins were laid
  On thee—alone on thee:
Thy precious blood our ransom paid;
  Thine all the glory be.

2 Shall we thy life of grief forget,
  Thy fasting and thy prayer,
Thy locks with mountain vapors wet,
  To save us from despair?

3 Gethsemane can we forget?
  Thy struggling agony,
When night lay dark on Olivet,
  And none to watch with thee?

165. *Temperance Hymn.* Sala. **8s & 6s.**

1 Friends of freedom, swell the song;
Young and old, the strain prolong;
Make the temperance army strong,
   And on to victory:
Lift your banners, let them wave;
Onward march a world to save:
Who would fill a drunkard's grave,
   And bear his infamy?

2 Shrink not when the foe appears;
Spurn the coward's guilty fears;
Hear the shrieks, behold the tears,
   Of ruined families.
Raise the cry in every spot,
"Touch not, taste not, handle not:"
Who would be a drunken sot? —
   The worst of miseries!

3 God of mercy, hear us plead;
For thy help we intercede:
Make the wretched drunkard blessed,
   By living soberly.
Raise the glorious watchword high —
"Touch not, taste not, till you die:"
Let the echo reach the sky,
   And earth keep Jubilee.

166. *Dismission.* Old Hundred. **L. M.**

1 Dismiss us with thy blessing, Lord;
Help us to feed upon thy word;
All that has been amiss forgive,
And let thy truth within us live.

2 Though we are guilty, thou art good;
Wash all our works in Jesus' blood;
Give every burdened soul release,
And bid us all depart in peace.

167. *Evening Hymn.* S. M.

1 The day is past and gone,
  The evening shades appear;
 O, may we all remember well
  The night of death draws near.

2 We lay our garments by,
  Upon our beds to rest;
 So death will soon disrobe us all
  Of what we here possess.

3 Lord, keep us safe this night,
  Secure from all our fears,
 Beneath the shadow of thy wings,
  Till morning light appears.

4 And if we early rise,
  And view th' unwearied sun,
 May we set out to win the prize,
  And after glory run.

5 And when our days are past,
  And we from time remove,
 O, may we in thy bosom rest,
  The bosom of thy love!

168. *Faith.*   Olivet.   6s & 4s.

1 My faith looks up to thee,
 Thou Lamb of Calvary,
  Saviour divine!
 Now hear me while I pray;
 Take all my guilt away;
 O, let me from this day
  Be wholly thine.

2 May thy rich grace impart
 Strength to my fainting heart,
  My zeal inspire;
 As thou hast died for me,
 O, may my love to thee
 Pure, warm, and changeless be —
  A living fire.

169. *Loving-Kindness.* L. M.

1 Awake, my soul, in joyful lays,
And sing thy great Redeemer's praise;
He justly claims a song from me;
His loving-kindness, O, how free!

2 He saw me ruined by the fall,
Yet loved me notwithstanding all;
He saved me from my lost estate;
His loving-kindness, O, how great!

3 Though numerous hosts of mighty foes,
Though earth and hell, my way oppose,
He safely leads my soul along;
His loving-kindness, O, how strong!

4 When trouble, like a gloomy cloud,
Has gathered thick, and thundered loud,
He near my soul has always stood;
His loving-kindness, O, how good!

5 I often feel my sinful heart
Prone from my Jesus to depart;
But though I have him oft forgot,
His loving-kindness changes not.

6 Soon shall I pass the gloomy vale,
Soon all my mortal powers must fail:
O, may my last expiring breath
His loving-kindness sing in death!

7 Then let me mount and soar away
To the bright world of endless day,
And sing with rapture and surprise
His loving-kindness in the skies.

170. *Prayer for a Blessing.* 8s, 7s, & 4s.

1 Come, thou soul-transforming Spirit,
Bless the sower and the seed;
Let each heart thy grace inherit;
Raise the weak, the hungry feed;
From the gospel
Now supply thy people's need.

171. *Forsaking all to follow Christ.* 8s & 7s.

1 Jesus, I my cross have taken,
  All to leave, and follow thee;
Naked, poor, despised, forsaken,
  Thou, from hence, my all shalt be;
And whilst thou shalt smile upon me,
  God of wisdom, love, and might,
Foes may hate and friends disown me;
  Show thy face, and all is bright.

2 Let the world despise and leave me;
  They have left my Saviour too;
Human hearts and looks deceive me —
  Thou art not, like them, untrue;
And whilst thou shalt smile upon me,
  God of wisdom, love, and might,
Foes may hate and friends disown me;
  Show thy face, and all is bright.

172. *Now, the accepted Time.* Walbridge. S. M.

1 Now is th' accepted time;
  Now is the day of grace;
Now, sinners, come without delay,
  And seek the Saviour's face.

2 Now is th' accepted time;
  The Saviour calls to-day;
To-morrow it may be too late;
  Then why should you delay?

3 Now is th' accepted time;
  The gospel bids you come,
And every promise in his word
  Declares there yet is room.

4 Lord, draw reluctant souls,
  And feast them with thy love;
Then will the angels swiftly fly
  To bear the news above.

173.   *Courage.*   8s & 7s.

1 Man may trouble and distress me;
  'Twill but drive me to thy breast:
Life with trials hard may press me;
  Heaven will bring me sweeter rest:
O, 'tis not in grief to harm me,
  While thy love is left to me;
O, 'twere not in joy to charm me,
  Were that joy unmixed with thee.

2 Go, then, earthly fame and treasure;
  Come, disaster, scorn, and pain;
In thy service pain is pleasure,
  With thy favor loss is gain.
I have called thee, Abba, Father,
  I have set my heart on thee;
Storms may howl, and clouds may gather;
  All must work for good to me.

174.   *Christian Fellowship.*   No Sorrow.   S. M.

1 Blest be the tie that binds
   Our hearts in Christian love;
 The fellowship of kindred minds
   Is like to that above.

2 Before our Father's throne
   We pour our ardent prayers;
 Our fears, our hopes, our aims are one,
   Our comforts and our cares.

3 We share our mutual woes,
   Our mutual burdens bear;
 And often for each other flows
   The sympathizing tear.

4 When we asunder part,
   It gives us inward pain;
 But we shall still be joined in heart,
   And hope to meet again.

175. *The Saint's Home.* Sweet Home. 11s.

1 'MID scenes of confusion and creature complaints,
　How sweet to my soul is communion with saints ;
　To find at the banquet of mercy there's room,
　And feel in the presence of Jesus at home.

Chorus.　Home, home ; sweet, sweet home,
　　　　Prepare me, dear Saviour, for glory, my home.

2 Sweet bonds that unite all the children of peace !
　And thrice precious Jesus, whose love cannot cease !
　Though oft from thy presence in sadness I roam,
　I long to behold thee in glory at home.

3 I sigh from this body of sin to be free,
　Which hinders my joy and communion with thee ;
　Though now my temptations like billows may foam,
　All, all will be peace when I'm with thee at home.

4 I long, dearest Lord, in thy beauties to shine,
　No more, as an exile, in sorrow to pine,
　And in thy dear image arise from the tomb,
　With glorified millions to praise thee at home.

176.　　　*Watching.*　　Ocean. 8s & 7s.

1 LIGHT of those whose dreary dwelling
　　Borders on the shades of death,
　Come, and by thy love's revealing
　　Dissipate the clouds beneath :
　The new heaven and earth's Creator,
　　In our deepest darkness rise,
　Scattering all the night of nature,
　　Pouring eye-sight on our eyes.

2 Still we wait for thine appearing :
　　Life and joy thy beams impart,
　Chasing all our fears, and cheering
　　Every poor, benighted heart :
　Come, and manifest the favor
　　Thou hast for the ransomed race ;
　Come, thou glorious God and Saviour,
　　Come, and bring thy gospel grace.

177. *Rejoicing in Hope.* **8s & 7s.**

1 Know, my soul, thy full salvation;
   Rise o'er sin, and fear, and care;
Joy to find, in every station,
   Something still to do or bear:
Think what spirit dwells within thee;
   Think what Father's smiles are thine;
Think what Jesus did to win thee:
   Child of heaven, canst thou repine?

2 Haste thee on from grace to glory,
   Armed by faith and winged by prayer;
Heaven's eternal day's before thee;
   God's own hand shall guide thee there:
Soon shall close thy earthly mission;
   Soon shall pass thy pilgrim days;
Hope shall change to glad fruition,
   Faith to sight, and prayer to praise.

178. *The Presence of Christ.* De Fleury. **8s D.**

1 How tedious and tasteless the hours
   When Jesus no longer I see!
Sweet prospects, sweet birds, and sweet flowers
   Have all lost their sweetness with me.
The midsummer sun shines but dim;
   The fields strive in vain to look gay;
But when I am happy in him,
   December's as pleasant as May.

2 His name yields the richest perfume,
   And sweeter than music his voice;
His presence disperses my gloom,
   And makes all within me rejoice.
I should, were he always thus nigh,
   Have nothing to wish for or fear;
No mortal so happy as I;
   My summer would last all the year.

179. *Song of Moses and the Lamb.* No Sorrow. S. M.

1 Awake, and sing the song
   Of Moses and the Lamb;
Wake, every heart and every tongue,
   To praise the Saviour's name.

2 Sing of his dying love;
   Sing of his rising power;
Sing how he intercedes, above,
   For us, whose sins he bore.

3 Sing, till we feel our heart
   Ascending with our tongue;
Sing, till the love of sin depart,
   And grace inspire our song.

4 Sing on your heavenly way,
   Ye ransomed sinners, sing;
Sing on, rejoicing every day,
   In Christ, th' eternal King.

180. *Encouraging Prospects.* 8s, 7s, & 4s.

1 Yes, we trust the day is breaking;
   Joyful times are near at hand;
God, the mighty God, is speaking,
   By his word, in every land:
      When he chooses,
   Darkness flies at his command.

2 While the foe becomes more daring,
   While he enters like a flood,
God, the Saviour, is preparing
   Means to spread his truth abroad:
      Every language
   Soon shall tell the love of God.

3 O, 'tis pleasant, 'tis reviving
   To our hearts, to hear, each day,
Joyful news from far arriving,
   How the gospel wins its way,—
      Those enlightening,
   Who in death and darkness lay.

181. *God leads us.* Greenville. 8s, 7s, & 4s.

1 Gently, Lord, O, gently lead us
  Through this lowly vale of tears;
 And, O Lord, in mercy give us
  Thy rich grace in all our fears.
   O, refresh us —
  O, refresh us with thy grace.

2 Though ten thousand ills beset us,
  From without and from within,
 Jesus says he'll ne'er forget us,
  But will save from every sin.
   Therefore praise him —
  Praise the great Redeemer's name.

3 O that I could now adore him,
  Like the heavenly host above,
 Who forever bow before him,
  And unceasing sing his love!
   Happy songsters,
  When shall I your chorus join?

182. *Morning at the Tomb.* Wilmot. 7s.

1 Morning breaks upon the tomb,
 Jesus scatters all its gloom!
 Day of triumph through the skies,
 See the glorious Saviour rise!

2 Christian! dry your flowing tears;
 Chase these unbelieving fears:
 Look on his deserted grave;
 Doubt no more his power to save.

3 Ye who are of death afraid,
 Triumph in the scattered shade;
 Drive your anxious cares away;
 See the place where Jesus lay!

4 Lo, the rising sun appears,
 Shedding radiance o'er the spheres;
 Lo, returning beams of light
 Chase the terrors of the night.

183. *Redeeming Love.* **7s.**

1 Now begin the heavenly theme;
    Sing aloud in Jesus' name;
    Ye who Jesus' kindness prove,
    Triumph in redeeming love.

2 Ye who see the Father's grace
    Beaming in the Saviour's face,
    As to Canaan on ye move,
    Praise and bless redeeming love.

3 Mourning souls, dry up your tears;
    Banish all your guilty fears;
    See your guilt and curse remove,
    Cancelled by redeeming love.

4 Hither, then, your music bring;
    Strike aloud each joyful string;
    Mortals, join the hosts above —
    Join to praise redeeming love.

184. *The Glory of Christ.* **11s & 8s.**

1 O Thou in whose presence my soul takes delight,
    On whom in affliction I call,
  My comfort by day, and my song in the night,
    My hope, my salvation, my all!

2 O, why should I wander an alien from thee,
    Or cry in the desert for bread?
  Thy foes will rejoice when my sorrows they see,
    And smile at the tears I have shed.

3 Ye daughters of Zion, declare, have you seen
    The Star that on Israel shone?
  Say, if in your tents my Belovéd has been,
    And where with his flock he has gone.

4 His lips as a fountain of righteousness flow,
    To water the gardens of grace;
  From which their salvation the Gentiles shall know,
    And bask in the smiles of his face.

185. *Cold Water.* Auld Lang Syne. C. M.

1 Shall e'er cold water be forgot,
  When we sit down to dine?
 Shall e'er cold water be forgot,
  Poured out by hand divine?
 From springs and wells it gushes forth,
  Poured out by hand divine;
 Poured out by hand divine, my friends,
  Poured out by hand divine.

2 To beauty's cheek, though strange it seems,
  'Tis not more strange than true,
 Cold water, though itself so pale,
  Imparts the rosiest hue.
 Yes, beauty in a water-pail
  Imparts the rosiest hue —
 Imparts the rosiest hue, my friends,
  Imparts the rosiest hue.

3 Then let cold water armies give
  Their banners to the air;
 So shall the boys, like oaks, be strong;
  The girls, like tulips, fair;
 The girls like tulips fair, my friends,
  The girls like tulips fair;
 The boys shall grow like sturdy oaks,
  The girls like tulips fair.

186. *Precious Name.* Captain Kidd. 6s.

1 How precious is the name!
  Brethren, sing, brethren, sing;
 How precious is the name!
  Brethren, sing, brethren, sing;
 How precious is the name
  Of Christ, the paschal Lamb,
 Who bore our guilt and shame
  On the tree, on the tree,
 Who bore our guilt and shame
  On the tree, on the tree!

187. *Place of Prayer.* Alps. **6s.**

1 Come to the place of prayer;
  The day is past and gone;
And on the silent air,
  The voice of praise is borne:
Sweet is the hour of rest,
  Pleasant the heart's low sigh;
The glow within our breast,
  And the hope beyond the sky.

2 Yes, tuneful is the sound
  Of converts as they sing;
Welcome the glory round,
  Shed from the Spirit's wing;
But bliss more sweet and still
  Than aught on earth e'er gave,
Our yearning souls shall fill
  In the world beyond the grave.

188. *The Bond of Love.* **8s & 6s.**

1 Our souls, by love together knit,
  Cemented, mixed in one,
One hope, one heart, one mind, one voice,
  'Tis heaven on earth begun.
Our hearts have oft within us burned,
  And glowed with sacred fire,
While Jesus spoke, and fed, and blessed,
  And filled th' enlarged desire.

Chorus. "A Saviour!" let creation sing;
  "A Saviour!" let the heavens ring;
'Tis God with us; we feel him ours;
His fulness in our souls he pours:
'Tis almost done, 'tis almost o'er;
  We'll join with those who've gone before;
We soon shall reach the blissful shore,
Where we shall meet to part no more.

189. *The Invitation and the Resolve.* **C. M.**

1 Come, weary sinner, in whose breast
  A thousand thoughts revolve;
 Come, with your guilt and fear oppressed,
  And make this last resolve:—

2 "I'll go to Jesus, though my sin
  Hath like a mountain rose;
 I know his courts; I'll enter in,
  Whatever may oppose.

3 "I'll prostrate lie before his throne,
  And there my guilt confess;
 I'll tell him I'm a wretch undone,
  Without his sovereign grace.

4 "Perhaps he will admit my plea,
  Perhaps will hear my prayer;
 But, if I perish, I will pray,
  And perish only there.

5 "I can but perish if I go;
  I am resolved to try;
 For if I stay away, I know
  I must forever die.

190. *Warfare.* **7s.**

1 What a Captain I have got!
 Is not mine a happy lot?
 Therefore we will take the sword,
 Fight for Jesus Christ our Lord.

Chorus. I his soldier sure shall be,
  Happy in eternity.

2 Brother soldiers, still fight on,
 Till the battle you have won;
 The great Captain you do choose,
 Never did a battle lose.

191. *Canaan.* Canaan. 8s & 10s.

1 TOGETHER let us sweetly live;
  I am bound for the land of Canaan;
In peace which none but Christ can give;
  I am bound for the land of Canaan.

Chorus. O Canaan, bright Canaan!
  I am bound for the land of Canaan;
O Canaan, it is my happy home;
  I am bound for the land of Canaan.

2 If you get there before I do, &c.
  Look out for me, I'm coming too, &c.
    O Canaan, bright Canaan, &c.

3 I have some friends before me gone, &c.
  And I'm resolved to travel on, &c.
    O Canaan, bright Canaan, &c.

4 Our songs of praise shall fill the skies, &c.
  While higher still our joys they rise, &c.
    O Canaan, bright Canaan, &c.

5 Then come with me, beloved friend, &c.;
  The joys of heaven shall never end, &c.
    O Canaan, bright Canaan, &c.

192. *Call to Sinners.* L. M.

1 RETURN, O wanderer, now return,
  And seek thy Father's face;
Those new desires which in thee burn
  Were kindled by his grace.

2 Return, O wanderer, now return;
  He hears thy humble sigh;
He sees thy softened spirit mourn,
  When no one else is nigh.

3 Return, O wanderer, now return;
  Thy Saviour bids thee live:
Come to his feet, and grateful learn
  How freely he'll forgive.

193.   *Parting Hymn.*   Bower of Prayer.

1 Farewell, my dear brethren; the time is at hand
That we must all part from this social band;
Our several engagements now call us away;
Our parting is needful, and we must obey.

2 Farewell, loving Christians, farewell for a while;
We'll soon meet again if kind heaven should smile;
And while we are parted and scattered abroad,
We'll pray for each other, and wrestle with God.

3 Farewell, ye young converts, who've listed for
Sore trials await you, but Jesus is near;   [war;
And though you must walk through this dark wilderness,
Your Captain's before you; he'll lead you to peace.

4 Farewell, weeping mourners, with sad, broken heart;
O, haste to know Jesus, and seek the good part;
He's full of compassion and mighty to save;
His arms are extended your souls to receive.

5 Farewell, careless sinner; for you we do mourn,
To think of your danger, and your unconcern;
You've heard of a judgment where all must appear;
O, there you'll stand trembling with tormenting fear.

6 The frolics and pastimes in which you delight
Will serve to torment you in that dreadful fright;
You'll think of the sermons which you've heard in
When hope's gone forever of hearing again. [vain,

7 Farewell, faithful pilgrims; farewell, all around;
Perhaps we'll not meet till the last trump shall
To meet you in glory I give you my hand, [sound;
The Saviour to praise in a pure social band.

194.   *Welcome.*   8s & 6s.

1 Amen, amen, my soul replies;
I'm bound to meet you in the skies,
  And claim my mansions there:
Now, here's my heart, and here's my hand,
To meet you in that heavenly land,
  Where we shall part no more.

195. *Salvation.* Salvation's free. **C. M.**

1 Salvation! O, the joyful sound!
　'Tis pleasure to our ears,
　A sovereign balm for every wound,
　　A cordial for our fears.

2 Buried in sorrow and in sin,
　　At hell's dark door we lay;
　But we arise, by grace divine,
　　To see a heavenly day.

3 Salvation! O, thou bleeding Lamb!
　　To thee the praise belongs:
　Salvation shall inspire our hearts,
　　And dwell upon our tongues.

4 Salvation! Let the echo fly
　　The spacious earth around,
　While all the armies of the sky
　　Conspire to raise the sound.

196. *Light in the Window.* **P. M.**

1 There's a light in the window for thee, brother,
　　There's a light in the window for thee;
　A dear one has moved to the mansions above;
　　There's a light in the window for thee.

Chorus. A mansion in heaven we see,
　　And a light in the window for thee;
　A mansion in heaven we see,
　　And a light in the window for thee.

2 There's a crown and a robe and a palm, brother,
　　When from toil and from care you are free;
　The Saviour has gone to prepare you a home,
　　With a light in the window for thee.

197. *Invitation.* Will you go? **L. M.**

1 We're travelling home to heaven above,
    Will you go? Will you go?
To sing the Saviour's dying love;
    Will you go? Will you go?
Millions have reached that blessed abode,
Anointed kings and priests to God,
And millions now are on the road;
    Will you go? Will you go?

2 We're going to see the bleeding Lamb,
In rapturous strains to praise his name:
The crown of life we there shall wear,
The conqueror's palms our hands shall bear,
And all the joys of heaven we'll share!
    Will you go? Will you go?

3 We're going to join the heavenly choir,
To raise our voice and tune the lyre;
There saints and angels gladly sing
Hosanna to their God and King,
And make the heavenly arches ring.
    Will you go? Will you go?

4 The way to heaven is free for all,
For Jew and Gentile, great and small;
Make up your mind, give God your heart,
With every sin and idol part,
And now for glory make a start.
    Come away! Come away!

5 The way to heaven is straight and plain;
Repent, believe, be born again;
The Saviour cries aloud to thee,
"Take up thy cross, and follow me,"
And thou shalt my salvation see.
    Come to me! Come to me!

198. *Free Salvation.* No Sorrow. **S. M.**

1 I'm glad salvation's free,
  I'm glad salvation's free;
  Salvation's free for you and me;
  I'm glad salvation's free.

199. *Jesus' Love.* 8s & 4s.

1 There's a friend above all others —
  O, how he loves!
His is love beyond a brother's —
  O, how he loves!
Earthly friends may fail and leave us,
This day, kind; the next, bereave us;
But this friend will ne'er deceive us —
  O, how he loves!

2 Love this friend who longs to save thee —
  O, how he loves!
Dost thou love? He will not leave thee —
  O, how he loves!
Think no more then of to-morrow;
Take his easy yoke and follow;
Jesus carries all thy sorrow —
  O, how he loves!

200. *Love to Jesus.* C. M.

1 Jesus, I love thy charming name;
  'Tis music to mine ear;
Fain would I sound it out so loud,
  That earth and heaven should hear.

2 Yes, thou art precious to my soul,
  My joy, my hope, my trust;
Jewels to thee are gaudy toys,
  And gold is sordid dust.

3 All my capacious powers can wish
  In thee most richly meet;
Nor to mine eyes is light so dear,
  Nor friendship half so sweet.

4 Thy grace still dwells upon my heart,
  And sheds its fragrance there;
The noblest balm of all its wounds,
  The cordial of its care.

201. *Our Refuge.* P. M. 7s.

1 Jesus, lover of my soul,
   Let me to thy bosom fly,
While the billows near me roll,
   While the tempest still is nigh.

2 Hide me, O my Saviour, hide,
   Till the storm of life is past;
Safe into the haven guide;
   O, receive my soul at last.

3 All my trust on thee is stayed,
   All my help from thee I bring;
Cover my defenceless head,
   With the shadow of thy wing.

4 Thou of life the fountain art;
   Freely let me take of thee;
Spring thou up within my heart—
   Rise to all eternity.

202. *Desiring Sanctification.* I love Jesus. 8s & 7s.

1 Love divine, all love excelling,
   Joy of heaven to earth come down,
Fix in us thy humble dwelling;
   All thy faithful mercies crown:
Jesus, thou art all compassion;
   Pure, unbounded love thou art;
Visit us with thy salvation;
   Enter every trembling heart.

2 Breathe, O, breathe thy Holy Spirit
   Into every troubled breast;
Let us all thy grace inherit;
   Let us find thy promised rest:
Take away the love of sinning;
   Take our load of guilt away;
End the work of thy beginning;
   Bring us to eternal day.

203. *Success of the Gospel.* Physician. 7s & 6s.

1 The morning light is breaking;
  The darkness disappears;
 The sons of earth are waking
  To penitential tears:
 Each breeze that sweeps the ocean
  Brings tidings from afar
 Of nations in commotion,
  Prepared for Zion's war.

2 Rich dews of grace come o'er us
  In many a gentle shower,
 And brighter scenes before us
  Are opening every hour:
 Each cry, to heaven going,
  Abundant answers brings,
 And heavenly gales are blowing,
  With peace upon their wings.

204. *Social Worship.* How happy. 11s & 8s.

1 How lovely the place where the Saviour appears,
  To those who believe in his word!
 His presence disperses my sorrows and fears,
  And bids me rejoice in my Lord.

2 A day in his courts, than a thousand beside,
  Is better and lovelier far—
 My soul hates the tents where the wicked reside,
  And all their delights I abhor.

3 Lord, give me a place with the humblest of saints,
  For low at thy feet I would lie;
 I know that thou hearest my feeble complaints;
  Thou hearest the young ravens' cry.

4 Give strength to the souls that now wait upon thee;
  O, come in thy chariot of love;
 From earth's vain enchantments, O, help us to flee,
  And to set our affections above.

205. *Heaven in Prospect.* Auld Lang Syne. C. M.

1 On Jordan's stormy banks I stand,
 And cast a wishful eye
To Canaan's fair and happy land,
 Where my possessions lie.

2 O the transporting, rapturous scene,
 That rises to my sight!
Sweet fields arrayed in living green,
 And rivers of delight.

3 No chilling winds, nor poisonous breath,
 Can reach that healthful shore;
Sickness and sorrow, pain and death,
 Are felt and feared no more.

4 When shall I reach that happy place,
 And be forever blest?
When shall I see my Father's face,
 And in his bosom rest?

206. *Titles of Christ.* Lenox. H. M.

1 Join all the glorious names
 Of wisdom, love, and power,
That ever mortals knew,
 Or angels ever bore,—
All are too mean | Too mean to set
To speak his worth, | The Saviour forth.

2 Great Prophet of our God,
 Our tongues shall bless thy name;
By thee the joyful news
 Of our salvation came,—
The joyful news | Of hell subdued,
Of sins forgiven, | And peace with heaven.

3 Jesus, our great High Priest,
 Has shed his blood and died;
Our guilty conscience needs
 No sacrifice beside:
His precious blood | And now it pleads
Did once atone, | Before the throne.

207. *Sinners entreated.* Greenville. 8s & 7s.

1 Come, ye sinners, poor and wretched,
    Come in mercy's gracious hour;
  Jesus ready stands to save you,
    Full of pity, love, and power:
      He is able —
  He is willing — doubt no more.

2 Let no sense of guilt prevent you,
    Nor of fitness fondly dream;
  All the fitness he requireth
    Is to feel your need of him:
      This he gives you;
  'Tis the Spirit's rising beam.

3 Agonizing in the garden,
    Lo, your Saviour prostrate lies;
  On the bloody tree behold him;
    There he groans, and bleeds, and dies;
      "It is finished;"
  Heaven's atoning sacrifice.

4 Lo, th' incarnate God, ascended,
    Pleads the merit of his blood;
  Venture on him — venture wholly;
    Let no other trust intrude:
      None but Jesus
  Can do helpless sinners good.

208. *Lord, remember me.* Pisgah. C. M.

1 O Thou, from whom all goodness flows,
    I lift my soul to thee;
  In all my sorrows, conflicts, woes,
    Good Lord, remember me.

2 When on my aching, burdened heart
    My sins lie heavily,
  Thy pardon grant, new peace impart;
    Good Lord, remember me.

3 When trials sore obstruct my way,
    And ills I cannot flee,
  O, let my strength be as my day;
    Good Lord, remember me.

209. *Pilgrim's Prayer.* Cross and Crown. 8s, 7s, 6s.

1 Eternal Spirit, on me move,
   While I am travelling here;
Lead me on to heaven above;
   O, have me in thy care:
Thou canst upon my heart now move,
   And fill me with thy perfect love,
All other love excelling.
      O, that's the love for me,
      O, that's the love for me,
      O, that's the love for me.

2 Fill me with thy fulness here,
   That I may holy be;
I'll cast away all worldly fear;
   May I thy glory see:
Grant me thy lovely, smiling face,
   And fill me with that perfect peace,
All worldly peace exceeding.
      For that's the peace for me,
      O, that's the peace for me,
      O, that's the peace for me.

210. *The Missionary's Farewell.* 8s, 7s, 4s.

1 Yes, my native land, I love thee;
   All thy scenes, I love them well:
Friends, connections, happy country,
   Can I bid you all farewell?
      Can I leave you,
   Far in heathen lands to dwell?

2 Home, thy joys are passing lovely—
   Joys no stranger-heart can tell;
Happy home, indeed I love thee:
   Can I, can I say, "Farewell"?
      Can I leave you, &c.

3 Scenes of sacred peace and pleasure,
   Holy days and Sabbath bell,
Richest, brightest, sweetest treasure,
   Can I say a last farewell?
      Can I leave you, &c.

211. *Morning Hymn.* Ortonville. **C. M.**

1 Lord, in the morning I will send
  My prayer to reach thine ear;
 Thou art my Father and my Friend,
  My help forever near.

2 O, lead me, keep me all this day
  Near thee, in perfect peace;
 Help me to watch, to watch and pray,
  To pray, and never cease.

3 So shall I pass all dangers safe,
  And tread the tempter down;
 My hope, my trust, joy and relief,
  Shall be in thee alone.

4 Thus let my moments smoothly run,
  And sing my hours away,
 Till evening shade and setting sun
  Conclude in endless day.

212. *Dying Happy.* **L. M**

1 Vital spark of heavenly flame,
 Quit, O, quit this mortal frame;
 Trembling, hoping, lingering, flying —
 O, the pain, the bliss of dying!
 Cease, fond nature, cease thy strife,
 And let me languish into life!

2 Hark! — they whisper — angels say,
 "Sister spirit, come away:"
 What is this absorbs me quite? —
 Steals my senses — shuts my sight —
 Drowns my spirits — draws my breath? —
 Tell me, my soul — can this be death?

3 The world recedes — it disappears —
 Heaven opens on my eyes! — my ears
  With sounds seraphic ring! —
 Lend, lend your wings! I mount! I fly!
 "O grave! where is thy victory!
  O death! where is thy sting!"

213. *Consideration.* 9s & 6s. **P. M.**

1 What a mercy, a mercy is this!
What a mercy, a mercy is this!
  What a mercy is this,
  What a heavenly bliss!
Jesus died to redeem a lost race!

2 What will, O, what will become of me,
What will, O, what will become of me,
  What will become of me,
  When death approaches me,
If the Saviour's not found in my heart?

3 'Tis awful, 'tis awful to relate,
'Tis awful, 'tis awful to relate,
  'Tis awful to relate,
  If death should be my fate,
If the Saviour's not found in my breast.

4 But welcome, but welcome, death, to me;
But welcome, but welcome, death, to me;
  If Christ should set me free,
  If Christ should set me free,
If my Saviour is found in my breast.

214. *Pardon penitently implored.* **L. M.**

1 Show pity, Lord; O Lord, forgive;
Let a repenting rebel live;
Are not thy mercies large and free?
May not a sinner trust in thee?

2 My crimes, though great, cannot surpass
The power and glory of thy grace;
Great God, thy nature hath no bound;
So let thy pardoning love be found.

3 O, wash my soul from every sin,
And make my guilty conscience clean;
Here, on my heart, the burden lies,
And past offences pain mine eyes.

4 My lips, with shame, my sins confess,
Against thy law, against thy grace;
Lord, should thy judgment grow severe,
I am condemned, but thou art clear.

215.   *Wonder.*   L. M.

1 When converts first begin to sing,
   Wonder, wonder, wonder,
 Their happy souls are on the wing,
   Glory, hallelujah.
 Their theme is all redeeming love,
   Glory, hallelujah!
 Fain would they be with Christ above,
   Sing glory, hallelujah.

2 With admiration they behold, &c.
 The love of Christ that can't be told; &c.
 They view themselves upon the shore, &c.
 And think the battle all is o'er, &c.

3 They feel themselves quite free from pain, &c.
 And think their enemies are slain; &c.
 They make no doubt but all is well, &c.
 And Satan is cast down to hell, &c.

4 They wonder why old saints don't sing, &c.
 And make the heavenly arches ring; &c.
 Ring with melodious, joyful sound, &c.
 Because a prodigal is found, &c.

216.   *The Jubilee.*   Salvation's free.   S. M.

1 Good news, good news to Adam's race;
  Let Christians all agree
 To sing redeeming love and grace;
  This is the Jubilee.

2 The gospel sounds a sweet release
  To all in misery,
 And bids them welcome home to peace;
  This is the Jubilee.

3 Jesus is on the mercy-seat;
  Before him bend the knee;
 Let heaven and earth his praise repeat;
  This is the Jubilee.

4 Sinners, be wise; return and come;
  Unto the Saviour flee;
 The Saviour bids you welcome home;
  This is the Jubilee.

217. *The World of Light.* **Joyful.**

1 Come, brethren, let us seek the Lord,
  And find in him a great reward.
  We'll each a starry crown receive,
  And reign above the sky.

1st Chorus. And reign above the sky,
  And reign above the sky,
  We'll each a starry crown receive,
  And reign above the sky.

2d Chorus. O, that will be joyful!
  Joyful, joyful!
  O, that will be joyful!
  To meet to part no more.

3d Chorus. To meet to part no more,
  On Canaan's happy shore;
  'Tis there we'll meet at Jesus' feet,
  Shall meet to part no more.

2 Come, let us travel on the way,
  Which leads to realms of endless day.
  We'll each a starry crown, &c.

3 Those holy joys, that blest abode!
  We shall be near and like our God.
  We'll each a starry crown, &c.

4 O, hallelujah, evermore,
  We'll sing on Canaan's happy shore.
  We'll each a starry crown, &c.

5 Angels above, who dwell in light,
  Sing praise to God with all their might.
  We'll each a starry crown, &c.

6 The ransomed saints will shout and sing,
  And make the heavenly arches ring.
  We'll each a starry crown, &c.

7 To Father, Son, and Holy Ghost,
  We'll shout, with all the heavenly host.
  We'll each a starry crown, &c.

8 While endless ages onward roll,
  Peace, like a river, fills the soul.
  We'll each a starry crown, &c.

218. *Sick Soul.* Funeral Bell. 6s & 5s.

1 Poor, sin-sick, weeping heart,
  What can relieve thee?
Come, sinful as thou art;
  Christ will receive thee.
Come, though with woe oppressed,
Soft is the Saviour's breast;
There mayst thou sweetly rest,
  Where nought shall grieve thee.

2 Come, trembling, timid soul;
  Why this delaying?
Thunders, that o'er thee roll,
  Fall on the straying.
Turn from destruction's ways;
Turn to the throne of grace;
There seek thy Father's face,
  Weeping and praying.

219. *Trembling Saints.* S. M.

1 Your harps, ye trembling saints,
  Down from the willows take;
Loud to the praise of love divine
  Bid every string awake.

2 Though in a foreign land,
  We are not far from home,
And nearer to our house above
  We every moment come.

3 His grace will to the end,
  Stronger and brighter shine;
Nor present things, nor things to come,
  Shall quench the love divine.

4 The time of love will come;
  Then we shall clearly see
Not only that he shed his blood,
  But each shall say, "For me."

220. *Baptismal Song.* Hotham. 7s.

1 Christians, if your hearts be warm,
Ice and snow will do no harm;
If by Jesus you are prized,
Rise, believe, and be baptized.

Chorus. And you've nothing for to fear;
Jesus Christ, your friend, is near;
Your friend is near, your friend is near;
Jesus Christ, your friend, is near;
And you've nothing for to fear;
Jesus Christ, your friend, is near.

2 Jesus drank the gall for you;
Bore the curse to sinners due;
Children, prove your love to him;
Never fear the frozen stream.
And you've nothing for to fear, &c.

3 Never shun the Saviour's cross;
All the earth is worthless dross;
If the Saviour's love you feel,
Let the world behold your zeal.
And you've nothing for to fear, &c.

4 Brave the tempest, storm, and tide,
Trusting to your heavenly guide,
Who will lead you by his grace
To his blessed resting-place.
So you've nothing for to fear, &c.

221. *Preciousness of the Bible.* C. M.

1 How precious is the book divine,
By inspiration given!
Bright as a lamp its doctrines shine,
To guide our souls to heaven.

2 This lamp, through all the tedious night
Of life, shall guide our way;
Life, light, and joy it still imparts,
And quells our rising fears.

222. *The Pilgrim's Song.* 7s, 6s, & 11s. P. M.

1 When I set out for glory,
  I left the world behind,
 Determined for a city
  (That's out of sight to find.)
Chorus. And to glory I will go,
  And to glory I will go, I'll go, I'll go,
  And to glory I will go.

2 Some said I'd better tarry;
  They thought I was too young
 For to prepare for dying;
  But that was all my theme.
    And to glory I will go, &c.

3 I left my young companions,
  And with them my good name;
 I left my earthly treasures,
  And all my worldly fame.
    And to begging I will go, &c.

4 Come on, my loving brethren,
  And listen to my cry;
 All you that are backsliders,
  Must shortly beg, or die.
    And to begging we will go, &c.

5 I do not beg for riches,
  Or to be dressed in fine;
 The garments Christ will give us
  The sun will not outshine.
    And to begging we will go, &c.

6 The richest man I ever saw
  Was one who begged the most;
 His soul was filled with Jesus,
  And with the Holy Ghost.
    And to begging we will go, &c.

7 But now we are encouraged,
  Come, let us travel on,
 Until we join the angels,
  And sing the holy song.
    And to glory we will go, &c.

223. *Funeral Bell.* 11s & 12s. P. M.

1 Far, far o'er hill and dell, on the winds stealing,
  List to the tolling bell, mournfully pealing:
Hark! hark! it seems to say, as melt those sounds away,
  So earthly joys decay, whilst new their feeling.

2 Now through the charméd air, on the winds stealing,
  List to the mourner's prayer, solemnly bending:
Hark! hark! it seems to say, Turn from those joys away,
  Life's joys and friendship's ray in the dark grave ending.

3 O'er a father's dismal tomb see the orphan bending,
  From the churchyard's gloom, hear the dirge ascending:
Hark! hark! it seems to say, How short ambition's sway,
  To those which ne'er decay, for life is ending.

4 So when our mortal ties death shall dissever,
  Lord, may we reach the skies, where care comes never;
And in eternal day, joining the angels' lay,
  To our Creator pay homage forever.

224. *Revival Day.* Wayfaring. L. M.

1 Ye new-born souls, your voices raise;
  Join to proclaim a Saviour's praise;
  Tell how he woke his saints to pray,
  And gave us this revival day.

2 O, it was cold, and dark, and drear,
  Till God the Comforter came near,
  Rent the thick cloud of gloom away,
  And brought this bright revival day.

3 Daughters of Zion, sons of God,
  Rise with melodious songs aloud;
  Tell to the world how blest are they
  Who share in a revival day.

4 O, sinners, cast your weapons down;
  Ye lukewarm, rouse; your folly own,
  And chant aloud Jehovah's praise,
  Who grants us these revival days.

225. *Happy Day.* **L. M.**

1 Preserved by thine almighty power,
 O Lord, our Maker, Saviour, King,
And brought to see this happy hour,
 We come thy praises here to sing.

Chorus. Happy day, happy day!
 Here in thy courts we'll gladly stay,
 And at thy footstool humbly pray,
 That thou wouldst take our sins away:
 Happy day, happy day,
 When Christ shall wash our sins away.

2 We praise thee for thy constant care,
 For life preserved, for mercies given;
O, may we still those mercies share,
 And taste the joys of sins forgiven.

3 We praise thee for the joyful news
 Of pardon through a Saviour's blood;
O Lord, incline our hearts to choose
 The road to happiness and God.

4 And when on earth our days are done,
 Grant, Lord, that we at length may join,
Teachers and scholars, round thy throne,
 The song of Moses and the Lamb.

226. *Christian Affection.* **L. M.**

1 How blest the sacred tie that binds
In sweet communion kindred minds!
How swift the heavenly course they run,
Whose hearts, whose faith, whose hopes are
 one!

2 To each, the soul of each how dear!
What tender love, what holy fear!
How doth the generous flame within
Refine from earth and cleanse from sin!

3 Nor shall the glowing flame expire,
When dimly burns frail nature's fire;
Then shall they meet in realms above,
A heaven of joy, a heaven of love.

227.   *A Revival.*   C. M.

1 Hark! hear the sound; on earth 'tis found;
  My soul delights to hear
How dying love, came from above,
  And pardon bought so dear.

2 God's ministers, like flaming fires,
  Are passing through the land;
The voice I hear, "Repent and fear;
  King Jesus is at hand."

3 God's people shine with grace divine;
  They're sanctified by truth;
The saints in prayer cry, "Lord, draw near;
  Have mercy on our youth."

4 Convinced of sin, men now begin
  To call upon the Lord;
Trembling, they pray, and mourn the day
  In which they scorned his word.

5 Young converts sing, and praise their King,
  And bless God's holy name;
While older saints, true penitents,
  Rejoice to join the theme.

6 God grant a shower of his great power
  On all those burdened hearts
That earnestly do mourn and cry
  That they may have a part.

7 From this glad hour exert thy power
  To melt each stubborn heart;
In those that bleed let love succeed,
  And holy joys impart.

8 Come, lovely youth, embrace the truth,
  And pray with one acord;
Saints, raise your songs, with joyful tongues,
  To hail th' approaching Lord.

228. *The Christian Race.* **C. M.**

1 Awake, my soul, stretch every nerve,
  And press with vigor on;
 A heavenly race demands thy zeal,
  And an immortal crown.

2 A cloud of witnesses around
  Hold thee in full survey;
 Forget the steps already trod,
  And onward urge thy way.

3 'Tis God's all-animating voice
  That calls thee from on high;
 'Tis his own hand presents the prize
  To thine uplifted eye; —

4 That prize, with peerless glories bright,
  Which shall new lustre boast,
 When victors' wreaths and monarchs' gems
  Shall blend in common dust.

229. *Salvation by Grace.* **C. M.**

1 Grace! 'tis a charming sound,
  Harmonious to the ear;
 Heaven with the echo shall resound,
  And all the earth shall hear.

2 Grace first contrived the way
  To save rebellious man;
 And all the steps that grace display,
  Which drew the wondrous plan.

3 Grace led my roving feet
  To tread the heavenly road;
 And new supplies each hour I meet,
  While pressing on to God.

4 Grace all the work shall crown,
  Through everlasting days;
 It lays in heaven the topmost stone,
  And well deserves the praise.

230. *Entreaty.* C. M.

1 With love and pity I look round
  Upon my fellow clay,
See men reject the gospel sound;
  Good Lord, what shall I say?

2 O, sinners, sinners, will you hear,
  When in God's name I come?
Upon your peril don't forbear,
  Lest hell should be your doom.

3 My bosom heaves o'er dying men,
  Doomed to eternal woe;
Fain would I speak, but 'tis in vain
  If God doth not speak too.

4 O, don't refuse to give him room,
  Lest mercy should withdraw;
He'll then in robes of judgment come
  To execute his law.

231. *Sinners exhorted.* P. M.

1 Child of sin and sorrow,
    Filled with dismay,
  Wait not for to-morrow,
    Yield thee to-day;
  Heaven bids thee come,
  While yet there's room;
  Child of sin and sorrow,
    Hear and obey.

2 Child of sin and sorrow,
    Why wilt thou die?
  Come, while thou canst borrow
    Help from on high:
  Grieve not that love
  Which from above,
  Child of sin and sorrow,
    Would bring thee nigh.

232. *Condition of the Heathen.* 7s & 6s.

1 From Greenland's icy mountains,
  From India's coral strand,
Where Afric's sunny fountains
  Roll down their golden sand,
From many an ancient river,
  From many a palmy plain,
They call us to deliver
  Their land from error's chain.

2 Shall we, whose souls are lighted
  By wisdom from on high,
Shall we to man benighted
  The light of life deny?
Salvation! O, salvation!
  The joyful sound proclaim,
Till earth's remotest nation
  Has learned Messiah's name.

3 Waft, waft, ye winds, his story,
  And you, ye waters, roll,
Till, like a sea of glory,
  It spreads from pole to pole;
Till o'er our ransomed nature
  The Lamb, for sinners slain,
Redeemer, King, Creator,
  In bliss returns to reign.

233. *Inquiry.* Shall we know each other? 8s & 7s.

1 When we hear the music ringing
  In the bright, celestial dome,
When sweet angel voices singing
  Gladly bid us welcome home
To the land of ancient story,
  Where the spirit knows no care,
In that land of light and glory,
  Shall we know each other there?

Chorus. Shall we know each other?
  Shall we know each other?
  Shall we know each other?
  Shall we know each other there?

234. *Anticipating Worship.* C. M.

1 Lord, in the morning thou shalt hear
  My voice ascending high;
 To thee will I direct my prayer,
  To thee lift up mine eye;—

2 Up to the hills where Christ is gone
  To plead for all his saints,
 Presenting at his Father's throne
  Our songs and our complaints.

3 O, may thy Spirit guide my feet
  In ways of righteousness,
 Make every path of duty straight
  And plain before my face.

235. *The good old Way.* L. M.

1 Lift up your heads, Immanuel's friends,
 And taste the pleasures Jesus sends;
 Let nothing cause you to delay,
 But hasten on the good old way.

2 Our conflicts here, though great they be,
 Shall not prevent our victory,
 If we but watch, and strive, and pray,
 Like soldiers in the good old way.

3 And when on Pisgah's top we stand,
 And view by faith the promised land,
 Then we will shout, and sing, and pray,
 And march along the good old way.

4 Ye valiant souls, for heaven contend;
 Remember life is at the end;
 Our God will wipe all tears away,
 When we have run the good old way.

5 When far beyond this mortal shore,
 We'll join with those who've gone before,
 And sing in yonder world of day,
 With all who've trod the good old way.

236. *Singing above.* Shall we sing. P. M.

1 SHALL we sing in heaven forever,
  Shall we sing?
Shall we sing in heaven forever,
  In that happy land?
Yes! O, yes! in that land, that happy land,
They that meet shall sing forever,
Far beyond the rolling river,
Meet to sing and love forever,
  In that happy land!

2 Shall we know each other ever,
  In that land?
Shall we know each other ever,
  In that happy land?
Yes! O, yes! in that land, that happy land,
They that meet shall know each other,
Far beyond, &c.

237. *Pilgrims.* Coming Home. C. M.

1 SING, all ye ransomed of the Lord,
  Your great Deliverer sing!
Pilgrims for Zion's city bound,
  Be joyful in your King!
Chorus. They're coming home, they're coming home,
  Behold them coming home,
  And saints and angels joy display
  O'er sinners coming home.

2 A hand divine shall lead you on
  Through all the blissful road,
Till to the sacred mount you rise,
  And see your smiling God.

3 March on in your Redeemer's strength,
  Pursue his footsteps still;
And let the prospect cheer your eye,
  While laboring up the hill.

238. *Sinners, will you.* Shepherd. 8s, 7s, & 4s.

1 Sinners, will you scorn the message
   Sent in mercy from above?
Every sentence, O, how tender!
   Every line is full of love;
      Listen to it —
Every line is full of love.

2 Hear the heralds of the gospel
   News from Zion's King proclaim
To each rebel sinner, "Pardon,
   "Free forgiveness, in his name;
      How important!
Free forgiveness in his name!

3 O, ye angels, hovering round us,
   Waiting spirits, speed your way,
Hasten to the court of heaven,
   Tidings bear without delay;
      Rebel sinners
Glad the message will obey.

239. *Praise to Christ.* L. M.

1 Join, all who love the Saviour's name,
To sing his everlasting fame;
Great God, prepare each heart and voice,
In him forever to rejoice.

2 With him I daily love to walk;
Of him my soul delights to talk;
On him I cast my every care;
Like him one day I shall appear.

3 Take him for strength and righteousness;
Make him thy refuge in distress;
Love him above all earthly joy,
And him in everything employ.

4 Praise him in cheerful, grateful songs;
To him your highest praise belongs;
Bless him who does your heaven prepare,
And whom you'll praise forever there.

240. *Sanctifying Influence.* **S. M.**

1 Come, Holy Spirit, come;
　　Let thy bright beams arise;
　Dispel the sorrow from our minds,
　　The darkness from our eyes.

2 Convince us all of sin;
　　Then lead to Jesus' blood,
　And to our wondering view reveal
　　The mercies of our God.

3 Revive our drooping faith,
　　Our doubts and fears remove,
　And kindle in our breasts the flame
　　Of never-dying love.

4 'Tis thine to cleanse the heart,
　　To sanctify the soul,
　To pour fresh life in every part,
　　And new-create the whole.

241. *Remission.* Happy Day. **L. M.**

1 O, HAPPY day, that fixed my choice
　　On thee, my Saviour and my God!
　Well may this glowing heart rejoice,
　　And tell its raptures all abroad.

2 O, happy bond that seals my vows
　　To Him who merits all my love!
　Let cheerful anthems fill his house,
　　While to that sacred shrine I move.

3 'Tis done, the great transaction's done;
　　I am my Lord's, and he is mine:
　He drew me, and I followed on,
　　Charmed to confess the voice divine.

4 High heaven, that heard the solemn vow,
　　That vow renewed shall daily hear;
　Till in life's latest hour I bow,
　　And bless in death a bond so dear.

242. *A Warning.* **P. M.**

1 O, HEARKEN; sinners, we have come
    To warn you of your danger;
  We pray be reconciled to Him
    Who once lay in a manger.

Chorus. Ho! every one that thirsts,
    Come ye to the waters;
  Freely drink and quench your thirst,
    O Zion's sons and daughters.

2 The awful God who made your soul,
    And all the world around you,
  Doth charge you with ten thousand crimes,
    But hateth to confound you.

243. *Loud Call.* **P. M. 7s & 6s.**

1 STOP, poor sinner, stop and think,
    Before you farther go;
  Can you sport upon the brink
    Of everlasting woe?
  Hell beneath is gaping wide,
    Vengeance waits the dread command,
  Soon will stop your sport and pride,
    And sink you with the damned.

Chorus. Then be entreated now to stop,
    For unless you warning take,
  Ere you are aware you'll drop
    Into the burning lake.

2 Say, have you an arm like God,
    That you his will oppose?
  Fear you not that iron rod,
    With which he breaks his foes?
  Can you stand in that great day,
    When his judgment he'll proclaim,
  When the earth will melt away
    Like wax before the flame?

244. *Difficulty and Dependence.* C. M.

1 Strait is the way, the door is strait,
  That leads to joys on high:
 They are but few who find the gate,
  While crowds mistake and die.

2 Belovéd self must be denied,
  The mind and will renewed,
 Passion suppressed, and patience tried,
  And vain desires subdued.

3 Lord, can a feeble, helpless worm
  Fulfil a task so hard?
 Thy grace must all the work perform,
  And give the free reward.

245. *Praising.* Ortonville. C. M.

1 In mercy, Lord, remember me
  Through all the hours of night,
 And grant to me most graciously
  The safeguard of thy might.

2 With cheerful heart I close my eyes,
  Since thou wilt not remove:
 O, in the morning let me rise,
  Rejoicing in thy love.

246. *Jesus' Name.* O, how I love Jesus. C. M.

1 Jesus, the name high over all,
  In hell, or earth, or sky:
 Angels and men before it fall,
  And devils fear and fly.

 Chorus. O, how I love Jesus;
    O, how I love Jesus;
    O, how I love Jesus;
    Because he first loved me:
    How can I forget thee?
    How can I forget thee?
    How can I forget thee?
    Dear Lord, remember me.

247. *Advent of Christ.* 8s & 7s.

1 HAIL, thou long-expected Jesus,
   Born to set thy people free!
From our sins and fears release us,
   Let us find our rest in thee.
Israel's strength and consolation,
   Hope of all the saints, thou art,
Long desired of every nation,
   Joy of every waiting heart.

2 Born thy people to deliver,
   Born a child, yet God our King,
Born to reign in us forever,
   Now thy gracious kingdom bring;
By thine own eternal spirit
   Rule in all our hearts alone,
By thine all-sufficient merit
   Raise us to thy glorious throne.

248. *Jesus our Intercessor.* 8s & 7s.

1 HAIL, thou once despiséd Jesus!
   Hail, thou everlasting King!
Thou didst suffer to redeem us,
   Thou didst free salvation bring.
Hail, thou agonizing Saviour,
   Bearer of our sin and shame!
By thy merits we find favor;
   Life is given through thy name.

2 Jesus, hail, enthroned in glory,
   There forever to abide!
All the heavenly hosts adore thee,
   Seated at thy Father's side;
There for sinners thou art pleading,
   There thou dost our place prepare,
Ever for us interceding,
   Till in glory we appear.

249. *God the Pilgrim's Guide.* **8s, 7s, & 4s.**

1 Guide me, O thou great Jehovah,
   Pilgrim through this barren land:
 I am weak, but thou art mighty;
   Hold me with thy powerful hand:
     Bread of heaven,
 Feed me till I want no more.

2 Open now the crystal fountain,
   Whence the healing streams do flow;
 Let the fiery, cloudy pillar
   Lead me all my journey through:
     Strong Deliverer,
 Be thou still my strength and shield.

3 When I tread the verge of Jordan,
   Bid my anxious fears subside;
 Bear me through the swelling current;
   Land me safe on Canaan's side:
     Songs of praises
 I will ever give to thee.

250. *The Closet.* Woodstock. **C. M.**

1 I love to steal a while away
   From every cumbering care,
 And spend the hours of setting day
   In humble, grateful prayer.

2 I love in solitude to shed
   The penitential tear,
 And all his promises to plead,
   Where none but God can hear.

3 I love to think on mercies past,
   And future good implore,
 And all my cares and sorrows cast
   On Him whom I adore.

4 I love by faith to take a view
   Of brighter scenes in heaven;
 The prospect doth my strength renew,
   While here by tempests driven.

251. *Watching for Souls.* **C. M.**

1 Let Zion's watchmen all awake,
   And take th' alarm they give;
Now let them from the mouth of God
   Their awful charge receive.

2 'Tis not a cause of small import
   The pastor's care demands,
But what might fill an angel's heart,
   And filled a Saviour's hands.

3 They watch for souls, for which the Lord
   Did heavenly bliss forego —
For souls which must forever live
   In rapture or in woe.

252. *Gratitude for Preservation.* **C. M.**

1 Come, let us strike our harps afresh
   To great Jehovah's name;
Sweet be the accents of our tongues
   When we his love proclaim.

2 'Twas by his bidding we were called
   In pain a while to part;
'Tis by his care we meet again,
   And gladness fills our heart.

3 Blest be the hand that has preserved
   Our feet from every snare,
And blest the goodness of the Lord,
   Which to this hour we share.

253. *Preachers.* **S. M.**

1 How beauteous are their feet
   Who stand on Zion's hill;
Who bring salvation on their tongues,
   And words of peace reveal!

2 How charming is their voice! —
   So sweet the tidings are;
Zion, behold thy Saviour King;
   He reigns and triumphs here.

254. *The Spirit's Power.* C. M.

1 Come, Holy Spirit, from above,
   With thy celestial fire;
Come, and with flames of zeal and love
   Our hearts and tongues inspire.

2 The Spirit, by his heavenly breath,
   New life creates within;
He quickens sinners from the death
   Of trespasses and sin.

3 The things of Christ the Spirit takes,
   And to our hearts reveals;
Our bodies he his temple makes,
   And our redemption seals.

255. *Purposes of God in Providence.* C. M.

1 God moves in a mysterious way
   His wonders to perform;
He plants his footsteps in the sea,
   And rides upon the storm.

2 Ye fearful saints, fresh courage take;
   The clouds ye so much dread
Are big with mercy, and shall break
   With blessings on your head.

3 Judge not the Lord by feeble sense,
   But trust him for his grace;
Behind a frowning providence
   He hides a smiling face.

256. *Prayer.* L. M.

1 Prayer is appointed to convey
   The blessings God designs to give:
Long as they live should Christians pray,
   For only while they pray they live.

2 The Christian's heart the prayer indites;
   He speaks as prompted from within;
The Spirit his petition writes,
   And Christ receives and gives it in.

257. *Zion's Beauty.* Beautiful Zion. 8s.

1 BEAUTIFUL Zion, built above;
  Beautiful city, that I love;
  Beautiful gates of pearly white;
  Beautiful temple,— God its light!
  He who was slain on Calvary
  Opens those pearly gates to me.

2 Beautiful crowns on every brow;
  Beautiful palms the conquerors show;
  Beautiful robes the ransomed wear;
  Beautiful all who enter there!
  Thither I press with eager feet;
  There shall my rest be long and sweet.

3 Beautiful throne for Christ our King;
  Beautiful songs the angels sing;
  Beautiful rest; all wanderings cease;
  Beautiful home of perfect peace!
  There shall my eyes the Saviour see:
  Haste to this heavenly home with me.

258. *Praying.* 7s.

1 NAY, I cannot let thee go
  Till a blessing thou bestow;
  Do not turn away thy face;
  Mine's an urgent, pressing case.
  Once a sinner, near despair,
  Sought thy mercy-seat by prayer;
  Mercy heard, and set him free!
  Lord, that mercy came to ME.

2 Many years have passed since then;
  Many changes have I seen,
  Yet have been upheld till now:
  Who could hold me up but thou?
  Nay, I must maintain my hold;
  'Tis thy goodness makes me bold;
  I can no denial take
  When I plead for Jesus' sake.

259. *Christian Unity.* H. M.

1 How beautiful the sight
  Of brethren who agree
 In friendship to unite,
  And bonds of charity !
'Tis like the precious ointment shed
O'er all his robes from Aaron's head.

2 'Tis like the dews that fill
  The cups of Hermon's flowers;
 Or Zion's fruitful hill,
  Bright with the drops of showers,
When mingling odors breathe around,
And glory rests on all the ground.

3 For there the Lord commands
  Blessings, a boundless store
 From his unsparing hands,
  Yea, life forevermore.
Thrice happy they who meet above,
To spend eternity in love.

260. *The Hope, the Star, the Voice.* C. M.

1 There is a hope, a blessèd hope,
  More precious and more bright
 Than all the joyless mockery
  The world esteems delight.

2 There is a star, a lovely star,
  That lights the darkest gloom,
 And sheds a peaceful radiance o'er
  The prospects of the tomb.

3 There is a voice, a cheering voice,
  That lifts the soul above,
 Dispels the painful, anxious doubt,
  And whispers, " God is love."

4 That voice, aloud from Calvary's height,
  Proclaims the soul forgiven;
 That star is revelation's light;
  That hope, the hope of heaven.

261.   *Warfare.*   Laban.   S. M.

1 O, watch, and fight, and pray;
  The battle ne'er give o'er;
Renew it boldly every day,
  And help divine implore.

2 Ne'er think the victory won,
  Nor lay thine armor down;
Thy arduous work will not be done
  Till thou obtain thy crown.

262.   *O that my Load.*   L. M.

1 O that my load of sin were gone!
  O that I could at last submit
At Jesus' feet to lay me down,
  To lay my soul at Jesus' feet!

2 Rest for my soul I long to find;
  Saviour of all, if mine thou art,
Give me thy meek and lowly mind,
  And stamp thine image on my heart.

3 Break off the yoke of inbred sin,
  And fully set my spirit free;
I cannot rest till pure within,
  Till I am wholly lost in thee.

263.   *The Lord provides.*   10s.

1 Though troubles assail, and dangers affright,
Though friends should all fail, and foes all unite,
Yet one thing secures us, whatever betide —
The Scripture assures us, the Lord will provide.

2 No strength of our own, nor goodness we claim;
Yet since we have known the Saviour's great name,
In this our strong tower for safety we hide, —
The Lord is our power, the Lord will provide.

3 When life sinks apace, and death is in view,
This word of his grace shall comfort us through;
No fearing or doubting, with Christ on our side,
We hope to die shouting, "The Lord will provide."

264. *The Sabbath welcomed.* **S. M.**

1 Welcome, sweet day of rest,
  That saw the Lord arise;
 Welcome to this reviving breast
  And these rejoicing eyes.

2 The King himself comes near,
  And feasts his saints to-day;
 Here we may sit and see him here,
  And love, and praise, and pray.

3 One day amid the place
  Where Christ, my Lord, has been,
 Is sweeter than ten thousand days
  Of pleasure and of sin.

4 My willing soul would stay
  In such a frame as this,
 Till called to rise and soar away
  To everlasting bliss.

265. *Justification by Faith.* **8s & 7s.**

1 Arise, my soul, arise;
  Shake off thy guilty fears;
 The bleeding Sacrifice
  In my behalf appears;
 Before the throne my Surety stands;
 My name is written on his hands.

2 The bleeding wounds he bears,
  Received on Calvary,
 Now pour effectual prayers,
  And strongly speak for me:
 "Forgive him, O, forgive," they cry,
 "Nor let that ransomed sinner die."

3 The Father hears him pray,
  The dear Anointed One;—
 He cannot turn away
  The pleading of his Son:
 His Spirit answers to the blood,
 And tells me I am born of God.

266. *Glorying.*   Ortonville.   **C. M.**

1 Ashamed of Christ! My soul, disdain
   The mean, ungenerous thought:
Shall I disown that Friend, whose blood
   To man salvation brought?

2 With the glad news of love and peace,
   From heaven to earth he came,
For us endured the painful cross,
   For us despised the shame.

3 At his command we must take up
   Our cross without delay;
Our lives — a thousand lives of ours —
   Can ne'er his love repay.

4 To bear his name, his cross to bear,
   Our highest honor this:
Who nobly suffers now for him
   Shall reign with him in bliss.

5 But should we in the evil day
   From our profession fly,
Jesus, the Judge, before the world,
   The traitor will deny.

267.   *Report of the Watchman.*   **7s.**

1 Watchman! tell us of the night,
   What its signs of promise are.
Traveller! o'er yon mountain's height
   See that glory-beaming star.

2 Watchman! does its beauteous ray
   Aught of hope or joy foretell?
Traveller! yes; it brings the day,
   Promised day of Israel.

3 Watchman! tell us of the night,
   For the morning seems to dawn.
Traveller! darkness takes its flight;
   Doubt and terror are withdrawn.

4 Watchman! let thy wanderings cease;
   Hie thee to thy quiet home.
Traveller! lo, the Prince of Peace,
   Lo, the Son of God, is come!

268. *The Worthies.* Hebrew Children. **P. M.**

Where now are the Hebrew children?
Where now are the Hebrew children?
Where now are the Hebrew children?
   Safe in the promised land:
They went up from a fiery furnace,
They went up from a fiery furnace,
They went up from a fiery furnace.
   Safe in the promised land.
By and by we'll go and meet them,
By and by we'll go and meet them,
By and by we'll go and meet them,
   Safe in the promised land.

2 Where now is John the Baptist?
   Safe in the promised land.
He went up from the river Jordan,
   Safe in the promised land.
By and by we'll go and meet him,
   Safe in the promised land.

3 Where now is good old Daniel?
   Safe in the promised land.
He went up from the den of lions,
   Safe in the promised land.
By and by we'll go and meet him,
   Safe in the promised land.

269. *The Spirit invoked.* **L. M.**

1 Come, sacred Spirit, from above,
And fill the coldest heart with love;
O, turn to flesh the flinty stone,
And let thy sovereign power be known.

2 O, let a holy flock await
In crowds around thy temple gate,
Each pressing on with zeal to be
A living sacrifice to thee.

270. *God seen in his Works.* Bethlehem. **L. M.**

1 The heavens declare thy glory, Lord;
　In every star thy wisdom shines;
But when our eyes behold thy word,
　We read thy name in fairer lines.

2 The rolling sun, the changing light,
　And nights and days, thy power confess;
But that blest volume thou hast writ
　Reveals thy justice and thy grace.

3 Nor shall thy spreading gospel rest
　Till through the world thy truth has run,
Till Christ has all the nations blest
　That see the light or feel the sun.

4 Great Sun of Righteousness, arise;
　O, bless the world with heavenly light;
Thy gospel makes the simple wise;
　Thy laws are pure, thy judgments right.

271. *Meditation at the Tomb.* Weep. **C. M.**

1 Hark! from the tombs a warning sound;
　My ears, attend the cry —
"Ye living men, come view the ground
　Where you must shortly lie.

2 "Princes, this clay must be your bed,
　In spite of all your towers;
The tall, the wise, the reverend head,
　Must lie as low as ours."

3 Great God, is this our certain doom?
　And are we still secure?
Still walking downward to the tomb,
　And yet prepare no more?

4 Grant us the power of quickening grace
　To fit our souls to fly;
Then, when we drop this dying flesh,
　We'll rise above the sky.

272. *God's Herald.* **P. M.**

1 Come, all ye mourning pilgrims, now,
　　The joyful news I'll tell;
　The Lord hath sent salvation down
　　To save our souls from hell.
　The angels brought the tidings down
　　To shepherds in the field,
　That God to man is reconciled,
　　His Son to man revealed.
　　　Sing glory, honor, to the Lamb,
　　　　Salvation to our King;
　　　All who are washed in Jesus' blood
　　　　His praises ever sing.

2 Come, all ye poor, despiséd souls,
　　Unto his fold repair,
　Where God his boundless love unfolds,
　　And says he'll meet us there.

273. *Parting.* We'll stem the Storm. **C. M.**

1 Yes, we part, but not forever;
　　Joyful hopes our bosoms swell;
　They, who love the Saviour, never
　　Know a long, a last farewell.
Chorus. We'll stem the storm; it won't be long;
　　　The heavenly port is nigh;
　　We'll stem the storm; it won't be long;
　　　We'll anchor by and by.

2 Sweet this hour of benediction,
　　When such unions come to mind,
　When each holy heart-conviction
　　Tells of bliss for us designed.
　　　We'll stem the storm, &c.

3 What a morrow beams before us!
　　Brighter far than tongue can tell!
　Glorious morrow to restore us
　　Him with whom we long to dwell.
　　　We'll stem the storm, &c.

274. *Baptism an Emblem.* **L. M.**

1 Do we not know that solemn word,
  That we are buried with the Lord?
 Baptized into his death, and then
  Put off the body of our sin?

2 Our souls receive diviner breath,
  Raised from corruption, guilt, and death;
 So from the grave did Christ arise,
  And lives to God above the skies.

3 With mind and heart I love the Lord,
  The brethren, prayer, and holy word,
 His Spirit and my soul attest,
  Till mighty grace shall give me rest.

275. *Following Christ.* **C. M.**

1 Buried beneath the yielding wave
  The great Redeemer lies;
 Faith views him in the watery grave,
  And thence beholds him rise.

2 Thus do his willing saints, to-day,
  Their ardent zeal express,
 And, in the Lord's appointed way,
  Fulfil all righteousness.

3 With joy we in his footsteps tread,
  And would his cause maintain, —
 Like him be numbered with the dead,
  And with him rise and reign.

276. *God our Portion.* **C. M.**

1 God, my supporter and my hope,
  My help forever near,
 Thine arm of mercy held me up,
  When sinking in despair.

2 Thy counsels, Lord, shall guide my feet
  Through this dark wilderness;
 Thine hand conduct me near thy seat,
  To dwell before thy face.

277. *The Lord's Supper instituted.* **L. M.**

1 "Do this," he cried, "till time shall end,
 In memory of your dying Friend;
Meet at my table, and record
 The love of your departed Lord.

2 "This is my body, broke for sin;
 Receive and eat the living food;"
Then took the cup, and blessed the wine;
 "'Tis the new covenant in my blood."

3 Jesus, thy feast we celebrate;
 We show thy death, we sing thy name,
Till thou return, and we shall eat
 The marriage supper of the Lamb.

278. *Communion with Christ.* Boylston. **S. M.**

1 Jesus invites his saints
 To meet around his board;
Here pardoned rebels sit, and hold
 Communion with their Lord.

2 This holy bread and wine
 Maintain our fainting breath,
By union with our living Lord,
 And interest in his death.

279. *The Gospel a Savor of Life or Death.* **C. M.**

1 Christ and his cross are all our theme;
 The mysteries that we speak
Are scandal in the Jew's esteem,
 And folly to the Greek.

2 But souls enlightened from above
 With joy receive the word;
They see what wisdom, power, and love,
 Shine in their dying Lord.

280. *Consoling.* 7s & 6s.

1 Come, my friend, and let us try,
  For a little season,
Every burden to lay by;
  Come, and let us reason.

2 What is this that casts you down?
  What is this that grieves you?
Speak, and let the worst be known;
  Speaking may relieve you.

3 Think on what your Saviour bore
  In the gloomy garden,
Sweating blood at every pore,
  To procure thy pardon.

4 View him nailéd to the tree,
  Bleeding, groaning, dying;
See, he suffered this for thee;
  Therefore be believing.

281. *Closing.* Greenville.

1 Lord, dismiss us with thy blessing;
  Fill our hearts with joy and peace;
Let us each, thy love possessing,
  Triumph in redeeming grace.
    O refresh us,
  Travelling through this wilderness.

2 Thanks we give, and adoration,
  For thy gospel's joyful sound;
May the fruits of thy salvation
  In our hearts and lives abound.
    May thy presence
  With us evermore be found.

3 So whene'er the signal's given,
  Us from earth to call away,
Borne on angels' wings to heaven,
  Called the summons to obey,
    May we ever
  Reign with thee in endless day.

1 Young people all, attention give,
　　While I address you in God's name;
　You who in sin and folly live,
　　Come, hear the counsel of a friend:
　I've sought for bliss in glittering toys,
　　I've ranged th' alluring scenes of life,
　But never found substantial joys
　　Until I heard my Saviour's voice.

2 He spake at once my sins forgiven,
　　And swept my load of guilt away;
　He gave me glory, peace, and heaven,
　　And led me in his own right way;
　And now with trembling sense I view
　　Huge billows roll beneath your path,
　While death eternal waits for you
　　Who slight the force of gospel truth.

3 Think of the soul where vengeance reigns!
　　It sinks in groans and ceaseless cries:
　It moves amidst the burning flames
　　In boundless woes and agonies;
　There swallowed up in blackest night,
　　Where devils dwell and thunders roar,
　To sink in keen despair and guilt,
　　When thousand thousand years are o'er.

4 O, fellow youth, this is the state
　　Of all who do free grace refuse;
　And soon with you 'twill be too late
　　The way of life in Christ to choose.
　Come, lay your carnal weapons by;
　　No longer fight against your Lord;
　And with my mission now comply,
　　And heaven shall be your great reward.

283.   *Christ precious.* I do believe.   C. M.

1 Jesus! delightful, charming name!
    It spreads a fragrance round;
  Justice and mercy, truth and peace,
    In union here are found.

2 He is our life, our joy, our strength;
    In him all glories meet;
  He is a shade above our heads,
    A light to guide our feet.

3 The thickest clouds are soon dispersed,
    If Jesus shows his face;
  To weary, heavy-laden souls
    He is the resting-place.

284.   *Heaven.*   C. M.

1 O, happy land! O, happy land!
    Where saints and angels dwell;
  We long to join that glorious band,
    And all their anthems swell.

Chorus. O, heaven, sweet heaven!
    O, home of the blest;
  How I long to be there,
  All its glory to share,
    And to lean on my Saviour's breast!

2 Be all our fresh, our youthful days
    To thy blest service given;
  Then we shall meet to sing thy praise,
    A ransomed band in heaven.

285.   *The Lamb of God.* The Cross. C. M.

1 Behold, behold, the Lamb of God
    On the cross, on the cross!
  For you he shed his precious blood
    On the cross, on the cross!
  The rocks do rend, the mountains quake,
  While Jesus doth atonement make —
  While Jesus suffers for our sake
    On the cross, on the cross.

286. *God's Goodness.* C. M.

1 What shall I render to my God
 For all his kindness shown?
My feet shall visit thine abode,
 My songs address thy throne.

2 Among the saints who fill thy house,
 My offering shall be paid;
There shall my zeal perform the vows
 My soul in anguish made.

3 How happy all thy servants are!
 How great thy grace to me!
My life, which thou hast made thy care,
 Lord, I devote to thee.

287. *Repentance.* L. M.

1 Return, my wandering soul, return,
 And seek an injured Father's face;
Those warm desires that in thee burn
 Were kindled by redeeming grace.

2 Return, my wandering soul, return;
 The dying Saviour bids thee live;
Go, view his bleeding side, and learn
 How freely Jesus can forgive.

3 Return, my wandering soul, return,
 And wipe away the falling tear;
'Tis God who says, "No longer mourn;"
 'Tis mercy's voice invites thee near.

288. *Christ's Invitation to Sinners.* L. M.

1 Come hither, all ye weary souls,
 Ye heavy-laden sinners, come;
I'll give you rest from all your toils,
 And raise you to my heavenly home.

2 Blest is the man whose shoulders take
 My yoke, and bear it with delight:
My yoke is easy to the neck;
 My grace shall make the burden light.

289. *Salvation by Christ.* Coronation. C. M.

1 Behold the sin-atoning Lamb,
 With wonder, gratitude, and love;
To take away our guilt and shame,
 See him descending from above.

2 Our sins and griefs on him were laid;
 He meekly bore the mighty load;
Our ransom-price he fully paid
 In groans and tears, in sweat and blood.

3 To save a guilty world he dies;
 Sinners, behold the bleeding Lamb;
To him lift up your longing eyes,
 And hope for mercy in his name.

290. *Jesus lives.* Old Hundred. L. M.

1 I know that my Redeemer lives;
What comfort this sweet sentence gives!
He lives, he lives, who once was dead,
He lives, my everlasting head.

2 He lives, and grants me daily breath;
He lives, and I shall conquer death;
He lives my mansion to prepare,
He lives to bring me safely there!

3 He lives, all glory to his name!
He lives, my Jesus, still the same;
O, the sweet joys the sentence gives,
I know that my Redeemer lives.

291. *Joyful Tidings.* Coronation. C. M.

1 Salvation! O, melodious sound
 To wretched, dying men!
Salvation that from God proceeds,
 And leads to God again.

2 My Saviour God, no voice but thine
 These dying hopes can raise;
Speak thy salvation to my soul,
 And turn my prayer to praise.

292. *Behold the Lamb of God.* **C. M.**

1 BEHOLD the Lamb of God, who bore
  Thy guilt upon the tree,
 And paid in blood the dreadful score,
  The ransom due for thee.

2 Behold him till the sight endears
  The Saviour to thy heart;
 His piercéd feet bedew with tears,
  Nor from his cross depart.

3 Behold him till his dying love
  Thy every thought control;
 Its vast, constraining influence prove
  O'er body, spirit, soul.

4 Behold him, as the race you run,
  Your never-failing Friend;
 He will complete the work begun,
  And grace in glory end.

293. *Buried with Christ by Baptism.* Greenville. **8s & 7s.**

1 THOU hast said, exalted Jesus,
  "Take thy cross and follow me;"
 Shall the word with terror seize us?
  Shall we from the burden flee?
   Lord, I'll take it,
  And, rejoicing, follow thee.

2 While this liquid tomb surveying,
  Emblem of my Saviour's grave;
 Shall I shun its brink, betraying
  Feelings worthy of a slave?
   No! I'll enter:
  Jesus entered Jordan's wave.

3 Blest the sign which thus reminds me,
  Saviour, of thy love for me;
 But more blest the love that binds me
  In its deathless bonds to thee:
   O, what pleasure,
  Buried with my Lord to be!

294. *Turtle Dove.* Bethlehem. **L. M. D.**

1 Hark! don't you hear the turtle dove,
A token of redeeming love?
From hill to hill we hear the sound;
The neighboring valleys echo round.
O, Zion, hear the turtle dove,
A token of redeeming love;
They've come these barren lands to cheer,
And welcome in the jubilee year.

2 The winter's past, the rain is o'er,
We feel the chilling winds no more;
Sweet spring has come, and summer too;
All things appear divinely new.
On Zion's mount the watchmen cry,
The resurrection's drawing nigh;
Behold, the nations from abroad,
Are flocking to the mount of God.

3 The trumpet sounds both far and nigh;
O, sinner, turn — why will you die?
Will you resist the gospel charms?
Come, list with Christ, gird on your arms.
These are the days that were foretold,
In ancient times, by prophets old;
They longed to see this glorious light;
But all have died without the sight.

4 The latter days have now come on,
And fugitives are marching home;
Behold, the nations from abroad
Are flocking to the mount of God.
O, yes, and I will join the band;
Here's my heart, and here's my hand;
With Satan's bands no more I'll be,
But fight for Christ and liberty.

295.   *The anxious Soul.*   P. M.

1 O, WHAT shall I do to be saved?
  Will you tell me, ye saints of the Lord?
 For long have I sought it with tears;
  But my weeping no rest can afford.

Chorus. O, I've sought it, I've sought it before,
  But I've sought it, I've sought it in vain;
 Yet I'll seek it, I'll seek it once more,
  Firmly hoping salvation to gain.

2 O, what shall I do to be saved?
  Can you tell me, that preach up the cross,
 If a sinner like me can be saved?
  On the billows of wrath I am tossed.

3 O, what shall I do to be saved?
  Can you tell me, young convert so strong?
 For I'm sinking in misery down,
  And in hell must awake before long.

4 Lord, what wilt thou have me to do?
  For my soul dies in anguish and pain!
 Men and brethren, my last look to you!
  Hell beneath moves my soul soon to gain.

5 "Believe and repent," saith the Lord;
  "Submit you to Christ," say the saints;
 "'Twas thus," says the convert, "I found
  Salvation from all my complaints."

296.   *Greeting.*   Auld Lang Syne.   C. M.

1 DEAR Saviour, we rejoice to hear,
  Poor sinners sweetly tell
 How thou art pleased to save from sin;
  From sorrow, death, and hell.

2 Lord, we unite to praise thy name,
  For grace so freely given;
 Still may we keep on Zion's road
  And dwell at last in heaven.

297. *Charity.* P. M.

1 Hail the gospel jubilee;
 Jesus comes to set us free,
 Who shed for us his precious blood,
 To raise our fallen souls to God;
 And since the work of suffering's done,
 We'll glory give to God alone.
 Free salvation be our boast,
 Ever mindful what it cost;
 Ever grateful for the prize,
 Let our praises reach the skies.

Chorus. Firm united let us be
 In the bonds of charity;
 As a band of brothers joined,
 Loving God and all mankind.

298. *Waiting.* German. 8s.

1 I'm glad that I was made to live;
 I'm on my way to glory;
 From sin and woe my soul shall go;
 I'm on my way to glory;
 I want to go, I long to go,
 I'm on my way to glory.

299. *No Sorrow there.* S. M.

1 Come, sing to me of heaven
 When I'm about to die;
 Sing songs of holy ecstasy,
 And waft my soul on high.

Chorus. There'll be no more sorrow there;
 There'll be no more sorrow there;
 In heaven above where all is love,
 There'll be no more sorrow there.

CHORUSES.

300. There are angels hovering round,
There are angels hovering round,
There are angels hovering round.

301. I will praise thee, I will praise thee;
Where shall I thy praise begin?

302. When I am happy I can sing,
I am on my journey home.

303. I am happy, I am happy,
I am happy in the Lord;
I don't want to stay forever here;
So freely, so freely, so freely,
Going home to glory.

304. May we all meet in heaven,
May we all meet in heaven,
Where we shall meet, at Jesus' feet,
To part no more.

305. Palms of victory, crowns of glory,
Palms of victory you shall bear;
Shout, O, glory, O, glory;
Palms of victory you shall bear.

306. There we shall see Jesus,
There we shall see Jesus,
There we shall see Jesus, Jesus, Jesus,
When we all shall meet above.

307. Glory, honor, praise, and power,
Be unto the Lamb forever!
Jesus Christ is our Redeemer!
Hallelujah! praise the Lord!

308. Hallelujah to the Lamb
 Who hath purchased our pardon;
We will praise him again
 When we pass over Jordan.

CHORUSES.

309. Turn to the Lord and seek redemption,
Sound the praise of his dear name;
Glory, honor, and salvation,
Christ the Lord has come to reign.

310. I am bound for the promised land,
I am bound for the promised land;
My Saviour smiles, and he bids me come;
I am bound for the promised land.

311. I am bound for the kingdom,
I am bound for the kingdom,
I am bound for sweet Canaan,
I am on my way home.

312. In this union, in this union,
We'll go on.

313. Home to glory, home to glory,
Home to glory, we will go.

314. He has been with us,
And he still is with us,
And he says he will go with us to the end.

315. I yield, I yield, I yield,
I can hold out no more.

316. O, he's taken my feet
From the mire and the clay,
And placed them on the rock of ages;
O, he's taken my feet
From the mire and the clay,
And placed them on the rock, Christ Jesus.

317. O, weep ye, weep, and mourn ye, mourn!
Forsake your evil way,
And to a righteous Judge return,
Before that dreadful day.

318. Brightest and best of the sons of the morning,
Dawn on our darkness and lend us thine aid;
Star of the East, the horizon adorning,
Guide where our infant Redeemer is laid.

319. Lord, revive us;
All our help must come from thee.

320. I love Jesus, Hallelujah,
I love Jesus, yes, I do;
I do love Jesus, he's my Saviour;
Jesus smiles, and loves me too.

321. Happy day, happy day,
When Jesus washed my sins away;
He taught me how to watch and pray,
And live rejoicing every day;
Happy day, happy day,
When Jesus washed my sins away.

322. Ho! every one that thirsteth,
Come ye to the waters,
Freely drink and quench your thirst,
Zion's sons and daughters.

323. For soon the reaping-time will come,
And angels shout the harvest home.

324. We're on our journey home
To the new Jerusalem.

325. Go on, go on; I'm bound to meet you in heaven;
I hope to meet you there,
Where parting is no more.

326. Good news gone to Canaan,
I'm on my way.

CHORUSES.

327. PRAISE ye the Lord, Hallelujah,
Hallelujah, praise ye the Lord.

328. I AM bound for the kingdom;
Will you go to glory with me?
Hallelujah, praise ye the Lord.

329. O, THE place, what a happy place,
The place where Jesus is.
The place where Christians all shall meet,
And never part again!

330. PRAISE, praise him, glory, Hallelujah.

331. I OWN I'm base, I own I'm vile,
But mercy's all my plea;
Remember, Lord, thy dying groans,
And then remember me.

332. O, SWEET heaven,
How I long to be complete!

333. O, WHO'S like Jesus? Hallelujah,
Praise ye the Lord;
There's none like Jesus! Hallelujah;
Love and serve the Lord.

334. COME, let us join our hearts and hands,
All in one band completely;
We're marching thro' Immanuel's land,
Where the waters flow so sweetly.

335. DON'T you hear th' archangels singing?
Hallelujah, Hallelujah.

336. O, TURN, sinners, turn;
May the Lord help you turn;
O, turn, sinners, turn; why will you die?

337. THY precious blood our ransom paid;
Thine all the glory be.

DOXOLOGIES.

338.   **L. M.**

    PRAISE God, from whom all blessings flow;
    Praise him, all creatures here below;
    Praise him above, ye heavenly host;
    Praise Father, Son, and Holy Ghost.

339.   **L. M.**

    To God the Father, God the Son,
    And God the Spirit, three in one,
    Be honor, praise, and glory given,
    By all on earth, and all in heaven.

340.   **C. M.**

    LET God the Father, and the Son,
        And Spirit, be adored,
    Where there are works to make him known,
        Or saints to love the Lord.

341.   **C. M.**

    To Father, Son, and Holy Ghost,
        One God, whom we adore,
    Be glory as it was, is now,
        And shall be evermore.

342.   **S. M.**

    YE angels round the throne,
        And saints that dwell below,
    Adore the Father, love the Son,
        And bless the Spirit too.

343.   **H. M.**

        To God the Father's throne
            Your highest honors raise;
        Glory to God the Son;
            To God the Spirit praise:
    With all our powers, eternal King,
    Thy name we sing, while faith adores.

INDEX TO FIRST LINES.

	HYMN
A beautiful land by faith I see	82
A charge to keep I have	72
Afflictions, though they seem severe	9
Ah, guilty sinner, ruined by transgression	47
Alas, and did my Saviour bleed	12
All hail the power of Jesus' name	63
All that I was, my sin, my guilt	18
Am I a soldier of the cross	83
Amen, amen, my soul replies	194
An alien from God, and a stranger to grace	41
A poor, wayfaring man of grief	123
Arise, my soul, arise	265
Ashamed of Christ! My soul disdain	266
As on the cross the Saviour hung	59
Awaked by Sinai's awful sound	14
Awake, and sing the song	179
Awake, my soul, in joyful lays	169
Awake, my soul, stretch every nerve	228
Attend, ye saints, and hear me tell	112
Baptized into our Saviour's death	149
Beautiful Zion, built above	257
Begone, unbelief; my Saviour is near	23
Behold a stranger at the door	16
Behold, behold, the Lamb of God	285
Behold the Lamb of God, who bore	292
Behold the sin-atoning Lamb	289
Be thou, O God, exalted high	97
Blest be the tie that binds	174
Blow ye the trumpet, blow	119
Broad is the road that leads to death	157
Brother, thou art gone to thy rest	91
Buried beneath the yielding wave	275
Child of sin and sorrow	231
Children of the heavenly King	163

INDEX TO FIRST LINES.

Christ and his cross are all our theme	279
Christians, if your hearts be warm	220
Come, all ye mourning pilgrims, now	272
Come and taste, along with me	56
Come, brethren, let us seek the Lord	217
Come, brethren, you that love the Lord	161
Come, Christian brethren, ere we part	145
Come, gracious Lord, descend and dwell	80
Come, heavenly love, inspire my song	1
Come hither, all ye weary souls	288
Come, Holy Spirit, Dove Divine	13
Come, Holy Spirit, heavenly Dove	5
Come, Holy Spirit, come	240
Come, Holy Spirit, from above	254
Come, let us strike our harps afresh	252
Come, my friend, and let us try	280
Come, sacred Spirit, from above	269
Come, sing to me of heaven	299
Come, sinners, to the gospel feast	103
Come, thou fount of every blessing	153
Come, thou soul-transforming Spirit	170
Come, — 'tis Jesus' invitation	99
Come to Jesus, come to Jesus	128
Come to the place of prayer	187
Come, trembling sinner, in whose breast	111
Come, weary sinner, in whose breast	189
Come, we that love the Lord	87
Come, ye disconsolate, where'er ye languish	62
Come, ye sinners, poor and wretched	207
Daughter of Zion, awake from thy sadness	53
Dear Saviour, we rejoice to hear	296
Did Christ o'er sinners weep	85
Dismiss us with thy blessing, Lord	166
Don't you see my Jesus coming	50
Do this, he cried, till time shall end	277
Do we not know that solemn word	274
Eternal Spirit, on me move	209

INDEX TO FIRST LINES.

Far, far o'er hill and dell, on the winds stealing	223
Farewell, dear friends, I must be gone	33
Farewell, dear friends, I must be gone	118
Farewell, farewell to all below	90
Farewell, my dear brethren, the time is at hand	193
Friends of freedom, swell the song	165
From every stormy wind that blows	105
From Greenland's icy mountains	232
From whence doth this union arise	155
Gently, Lord, O, gently lead us	181
God is love; his mercy brightens	36
God moves in a mysterious way	255
God, my supporter and my hope	276
Good news, good news to Adam's race	216
Go, teach the nations, and baptize	140
Grace! 'tis a charming sound	229
Great Jehovah, we adore thee	127
Guide me, O thou great Jehovah	249
Hail, sovereign love, that first began	48
Hail, sweetest, dearest tie that binds	79
Hail the blest morn! see the great Mediator	61
Hail the gospel jubilee	297
Hail, thou long-expected Jesus	247
Hail, thou once despiséd Jesus	248
Hark! don't you hear the turtle dove	294
Hark! from the tombs a warning sound	271
Hark! hark! the gospel trumpet sounds	109
Hark! hear the sound; on earth 'tis found	227
Hark! the voice of love and mercy	95
Hear the royal proclamation	116
Heart of stone, relent, relent	88
Holy Ghost, with light divine	159
Holy Source of consolation	130
How beauteous are their feet	253
How beautiful the sight	259
How blest the sacred tie that binds	226
How firm a foundation, ye saints of the Lord	43

How happy is the Christian's state	162
How lovely the place where the Saviour appears	204
How lost was my condition	101
How precious is the name	186
How precious is the book divine	221
How sweet to reflect on those joys that await me	57
How sweet the name of Jesus sounds	134
How tedious and tasteless the hours	178
I have fought the good fight	42
I know that my Redeemer lives	158
I know that my Redeemer lives	290
I'll try to prove faithful	154
I love thee, I love thee, I love thee, my Lord	60
I love to steal a while away	250
I'm a pilgrim, and I'm a stranger	17
I'm a pilgrim, and I'm a stranger	31
I'm glad salvation's free	198
I'm glad that I was born to die	132
I'm glad that I was made to live	298
I'm not ashamed to own my Lord	25
In all my Lord's appointed ways	8
In Jordan's tide the Baptist stands	71
In mercy, Lord, remember me	245
Inquire, ye pilgrims, for the way	11
Inscribed upon the cross we see	19
In the Christian's home in glory	106
In the cross of Christ I glory	137
In thy name, O Lord, assembling	49
I want to be an angel	136
I would not live alway: I ask not to stay	35
Jerusalem, my happy home	138
Jesus, and shall it ever be	29
Jesus, dear name, how sweet the sound	30
Jesus! delightful, charming name	283
Jesus, I my cross have taken	171
Jesus, I love thy charming name	200
Jesus invites his saints	278

INDEX TO FIRST LINES.

Jesus, lover of my soul	201
Jesus, my all, to heaven is gone	139
Jesus, my truth, my way	125
Jesus, the name high over all	246
Jesus, thou art the sinner's friend	117
Jesus, thy love shall we forget	164
Jesus, where'er thy people meet	66
Join all the glorious names	206
Join, all who love the Saviour's name	239
Joyfully, joyfully onward I move	74
Just as I am, without one plea	40
Know, my soul, thy full salvation	177
Let God the Father, and the Son	340
Let thy kingdom, blesséd Saviour	152
Let Zion's watchmen all awake	251
Lift up your heads, Immanuel's friends	235
Light of those whose dreary dwelling	176
Lo! on a narrow neck of land	143
Lord, dismiss us with thy blessing	281
Lord, in the morning I will send	211
Lord, in the morning thou shalt hear	234
Love divine, all love excelling	202
Man may trouble and distress me	173
Mary to the Saviour's tomb	34
Meekly in Jordan's holy stream	113
Mercy, O thou son of David	141
Met, O God, to ask thy presence	122
'Mid scenes of confusion and creature complaints	175
Morning breaks upon the tomb	182
Must Jesus bear the cross alone	150
My Bible leads to glory	146
My brother, I wish you well	148
My country, 'tis of thee	126
My faith looks up to thee	168
My heavenly home is bright and fair	84
My heavenly home is bright and fair	142

My pilgrimage will shortly end	51
My soul's full of glory, inspiring my tongue	147
Nay, I cannot let thee go	258
Nearer, my God, to thee	86
Nothing, either great or small	55
Now begin the heavenly theme	183
Now is th' accepted time	172
Now the Saviour standeth pleading	38
O, come, my loving neighbors, will you go to glory	93
O for a breeze of heavenly love	2
O for a closer walk with God	89
O for a thousand tongues to sing	32
O, happy day, that fixed my choice	241
O, happy land! O, happy land	284
O, hearken; sinners, we have come	242
O, how happy are they	73
O, land of rest, for thee I sigh	110
O Jesus, my Saviour, to thee I submit	76
O Lord, thy work revive	96
On Jordan's stormy banks I stand	205
O that my load of sin were gone	262
O, there will be mourning, mourning, mourning	75
O Thou, from whom all goodness flows	208
O Thou in whose presence my soul takes delight	184
O, turn ye, O, turn ye, for why will you die	20
Our Captain leads us on	133
Our souls, by love together knit	188
Out on an ocean all boundless we ride	52
O, watch, and fight, and pray	261
O, what shall I do to be saved	295
O, when shall I see Jesus	15
O, ye young, ye gay, and proud	65
Poor sin-sick, weeping heart	218
Prayer is appointed to convey	256
Prayer is the contrite sinner's voice	156
Prayer is the soul's sincere desire	144

INDEX TO FIRST LINES.

Pray on, my brethren in the Lord	151
Precious Bible! what a treasure	10
Preserved by thine almighty power	225
Religion is the chief concern	6
Remember, sinful youth, you must die	107
Return, return, my wandering soul	287
Return, O wanderer, now return	192
Rock of ages, cleft for me	104
Salvation, O, melodious sound	291
Salvation, O, the joyful sound	195
Saviour, visit thy plantation	115
Saw ye my Saviour, saw ye my Saviour	70
Say, brothers, will you meet us	114
Shall e'er cold water be forgot	185
Shall we meet beyond the river	24
Shall we sing in heaven forever	236
Show pity, Lord; O Lord, forgive	214
Since man by sin hast lost his God	124
Sing, all ye ransomed of the Lord	237
Sinners, will you scorn the message	238
Soldiers of the cross, arise	94
Sovereign grace has power alone	131
Stop, poor sinner, stop and think	243
Strait is the way, the door is strait	244
Sweet hour of prayer, sweet hour of prayer	58
That awful day will surely come	39
The day is past and gone	167
The happy morn is come	129
The heavens declare thy glory, Lord	270
The Lord into his garden comes	121
The Lord is my Shepherd, no want shall I know	69
The Lord is our shepherd, our guardian and guide	64
The morning light is breaking	203
There is a fountain filled with blood	54
There is a hope, a bless´ed hope	260
There is a land of pure delight	45

INDEX TO FIRST LINES.

There's a friend above all others	199
There's a light in the window for thee, brother	196
There is an hour of peaceful rest	100
The sovereign will of God alone	92
The voice of free grace cries, Escape	22
Though troubles assail, and dangers affright	263
Thou hast said, exalted Jesus	293
Thou sweet gliding Kedron, thy silver streams	58
To-day, if you will hear his voice	67
Together let us sweetly live	191
To leave my dear friends, and with neighbors to part	37
Vain, delusive world, adieu	160
Vital spark of heavenly flame	212
Watchman! tell us of the night	267
We all must speak for Jesus	26
Welcome sweet day of rest	264
We're travelling home to heaven above	197
What a Captain I have got	190
What a mercy, a mercy is this	213
What shall I render to my God	186
What's this that steals, that steals upon my frame	27
What various hindrances we meet	3
When all thy mercies, O my God	135
When converts first begin to sing	215
When I can read my title clear	46
When I set out for glory	222
When I was down in Egypt land	120
When marshalled on the nightly plain	81
When torn is the bosom with sorrow or care	102
When thou, my righteous Judge	21
When we hear the music ringing	233
Whene'er we meet, you always say	28
Where now are the Hebrew children	268
While nature was sinking in stillness to rest	77
With love and pity I look round	230
Whither goest thou, pilgrim stranger	44

INDEX TO FIRST LINES.

Why should the children of a king . . . 78
Why sleep we, my brethren? come, let us arise . 7

Ye dying sons of men 98
Ye new-born souls, your voices raise . . . 224
Yes, my native land I love thee 210
Yes, we part, but not forever 273
Yes, we trust the day is breaking . . . 180
Ye valiant soldiers of the cross 4
Young people all, attention give . . . 282
Your harps, ye trembling saints 219
You will see your Lord a coming . . . 105

CHORUSES.

Brightest and best of the sons 318

Come, let us join our hearts and hands . . 334

Don't you hear the archangels 335

For soon the reaping time 323

Glory, honor, praise, and 307
Good news gone to Canaan 326
Go on, go on; I'm bound to 325

Hallelujah to the Lamb 308
Happy day, happy day 321
He has been with us 314
Ho! every one that thirsteth 322
Home to glory, home to glory 313

I am bound for the kingdom 311
I am bound for the kingdom 323
I am bound for the promised land . . . 310
I am happy, I am happy 303
I love Jesus, Hallelujah 320

INDEX TO FIRST LINES.

In this union	312
I own I'm base	331
I will praise thee	301
I yield, I yield	315
Lord, revive us	319
May we all meet	304
O, he's taken my feet	316
O, sweet heaven	332
O, the place, what	329
O, turn, sinners	336
O, weep ye, weep	317
O, who's like Jesus	333
Palms of victory	305
Praise, praise him	330
Praise ye the Lord	327
There are angels hovering round	300
There we shall see Jesus	306
Thy precious blood	337
Turn to the Lord	309
When I am happy	303
We're on our journey	324

DOXOLOGIES.

Let God the Father	340
Praise God, from whom	338
To Father, Son, and	341
To God the Father, God	339
To God the Father's throne	343
Ye angels round	342

www.ingramcontent.com/pod-product-compliance
Lightning Source LLC
Chambersburg PA
CBHW032157160426
43197CB00008B/954